Farrand & Co.'s Premium Edition.

A

POCKET DICTIONARY

OF

THE LAW

OF

BILLS OF EXCHANGE, PROMISSORY NOTES, BANK NOTES, CHECKS, &c.

WITH

AN APPENDIX,

CONTAINING

ABSTRACTS OF ACTS AND SELECT CASES

RELATIVE TO

Negotiable Securities,

ANALYSIS OF A COUNT IN ASSUMPSIT,

TABLES OF NOTARIAL FEES, STAMPS, POSTAGE, &c.

BY JOHN IRWING MAXWELL, ESQ.
Of the honourable Society of the Inner Temple, Author of
" The Spirit of Marine Law," &c.

WITH MANY ADDITIONS
FOR THE USE OF THE AMERICAN MERCHANT.

THE LAWBOOK EXCHANGE, LTD.
Clark, New Jersey

ISBN 978-1-58477-312-2

Lawbook Exchange edition 2004, 2020

The quality of this reprint is equivalent to the quality of the original work.

THE LAWBOOK EXCHANGE, LTD.
33 Terminal Avenue
Clark, New Jersey 07066-1321

*Please see our website for a selection of our other publications
and fine facsimile reprints of classic works of legal history:*
www.lawbookexchange.com

Library of Congress Cataloging-in-Publication Data

Maxwell, John Irving.
    A pocket dictionary of the law of bills of exchange, promissory
notes, bank notes, checks, & c. : with an appendix, containing abstracts of acts
and select cases relative to negotiable securities, analysis of a count in assumpsit,
tables of notarial fees, stamps, postage, &c./ by John Irving Maxwell ; with
many additions for the use of the American merchant.
        p. cm.
    "Farrand & Co.'s premium edition."
    Originally published: Philadelphia : William P. Farrand and co., 1808.
    Includes bibliographical references.
    ISBN 1-58477-312-X (cloth: alk. paper)
    1. Negotiable instruments—Great Britain. I. Title.

KD1695 .M39 2003
346.41'096—dc2l   2002044362

Printed in the United States of America on acid-free paper

Farrand & Co.'s Premium Edition.

A

POCKET DICTIONARY

OF

THE LAW

OF

BILLS OF EXCHANGE, PROMISSORY NOTES, BANK NOTES, CHECKS, &c.

WITH

AN APPENDIX,

CONTAINING

ABSTRACTS OF ACTS AND SELECT CASES

RELATIVE TO

𝕹𝖊𝖌𝖔𝖙𝖎𝖆𝖇𝖑𝖊 𝕾𝖊𝖈𝖚𝖗𝖎𝖙𝖎𝖊𝖘,

ANALYSIS OF A COUNT IN ASSUMPSIT,

TABLES OF NOTARIAL FEES, STAMPS, POSTAGE, &c.

BY JOHN IRWING MAXWELL, ESQ.

Of the honourable Society of the Inner Temple, Author of
" The Spirit of Marine Law," &c.

WITH MANY ADDITIONS
FOR THE USE OF THE AMERICAN MERCHANT.

PHILADELPHIA:
PUBLISHED BY WILLIAM P. FARRAND AND CO.
1808.

TO THE PUBLIC.

In order to insure correctness the publishers of this book have subjected it to a critical examination in the following manner—Two proof sheets have been put up for public examination; one at the publishers' counting-house, the other at the city library in Philadelphia, and a premium of one dollar has been offered for every error that might be discovered: hence it is designated a *pre-mium* edition.

PRINTED BY FRY AND KAMMERER,
Printers of Farrand and Co.'s Premium Editions.

TO

DAVID SCOTT, ESQ.

A GENTLEMAN,
FROM WHOSE KNOWLEDGE AND EXERTIONS
IN THE MOST VALUABLE BRANCH OF
NATIONAL COMMERCE,
THE EAST INDIA COMPANY, AND THE PUBLIC,
HAVE DERIVED IMPORTANT ADVANTAGES;

A GENTLEMAN, WHO,
WITH ALL THAT CONSTITUTES EXCELLENCE IN
THE MERCANTILE CHARACTER,
COMBINES
THE AMIABLE QUALITIES OF INDIVIDUAL WORTH;

THIS COMMERCIAL ESSAY
IS MOST RESPECTFULLY INSCRIBED
BY THE AUTHOR.

PRELIMINARY ESSAY.

THE celebrated writer of the Spirit of Laws has remarked, that attention to commerce is the specific character of British policy. "In every other country (says that enlightened author), commerce is made subservient to politics; in Great Britain politics are made subservient to commerce." To this wise policy may be justly attributed the proud pre-eminence which this country has attained; to this her internal splendour, to this her external consequence, to this that aggrandisement which renders the figure in the speech of the Scythian philosophers to Alexander no longer an hyperbole; of Great Britain it may be truly said, "with her right hand she reaches

Asia,

Asia, with her left she lays hold of Europe."

Freedom, and protection of commerce,
constitute the very essence of the British
constitution. The protection of merchant
strangers was the express object of some
of our most ancient laws. All that legis-
lative wisdom could plan, or well-directed
power execute, have infused their energies
into the vast machine of commercial operation, and it may be truly observed, that
in no country under heaven has so much
attention been devoted to promote and
bring to perfection the reciprocal facilities
of commercial intercourse.

Subjects of states independent of each
other, amenable only to the laws of their
respective governments, and owing merely
a local allegiance during their temporary
presence in any foreign state, the multi-
tudinous body of merchants, varying in
customs, language, habits, and manners,
connected only by the common bond of
reciprocity

reciprocity of interest, will naturally select as a central point of communication that country whose equitable laws are framed with the strictest regard to commercial relations and individual rights. Such are precisely the laws of this country; and national wealth, splendour, and aggrandisement have been the result of this enlightened policy; here commerce has erected her throne, here she may truly be said " to reign, and here to revel."

To trace progressively the gradations by which Great Britain has attained this commercial pre-eminence, however interesting or gratifying to curiosity such an effort might prove, is nevertheless not within the scope of a publication from which theory is excluded, and in which practical utility is the only object; the following brief observations will be offered.

Without reverting to the Lombard Jews, or the Romans in the time of Cicero, for the origin of bills of exchange, it may be observed,

observed, that foreign bills appear to have been introduced into this country about the year 1381. Upon the first introduction of these instruments the Courts would only give effect to bills made between English merchants and merchant strangers. At this period commerce was in its infancy; advancing in progress a more extensive latitude was required. As commercial intercourse became more extensive, regulations commensurate with such progressive extension became necessary, and bills between merchants resident within this realm became reciprocally current.

Without attempting to trace the precise period when inland bills were first introduced, it will only be observed, that these became customary in the reign of Charles II. an æra when the most important commercial regulations were projected.

Although from the exigencies of a flourishing internal trade it became equally necessary to facilitate the intercourse between

tween British merchants resident within the country, as that between British and foreign merchants, and consequently that inland bills should be entitled to the same currency and privileges as foreign; yet in legal construction they were not so favoured, and various cases occur in the books with respect to the allowance of days of grace and other points of distinction, until at length the legislature, by the acts of William and Mary and Queen Anne, expressly extended the privileges of foreign to inland bills of exchange.

Promissory notes, which are of much more recent origin, were, like inland bills, upon their first introduction, subject to various litigations. These instruments, equally necessary for the purposes of internal trade as inland bills, were not at first considered by our Courts as negotiable instruments within the custom of merchants. Lord Chief Justice Holt would allow to a promissory note no intrinsic va-

lidity;

lidity; he considered it only as evidence of
a debt, and that the party had no remedy
but against the person from whom he immediately received it. In consequence of
this opinion, and an application to the legislature by several respectable merchants,
the statute of Queen Anne was passed, the
preamble to which recites the great advantages that would be derived to commerce
from putting promissory notes upon a footing with bills of exchange, and by the
enacting part of the act these instruments
construed in future to take effect exactly
similar to Bills of exchange.

Notwithstanding this statute, however,
the spirit of which could not be easily mis-
conceived, and the words of which appear
to contain no loop nor hinge to hang a
doubt upon, yet it was doubted whether
promissory notes should, like bills of exchange, be entitled to days of grace, and
in other points of resemblance where the
legislature had determined to identify, the
Courts

Courts seemed inclined to distinguish. In these times, indeed, judges were not so conversant with commercial subjects as their enlightened successors, and commercial jurisprudence, not only in this but in other branches, was not so well understood; cases were decided without adherence to established principle, jarring decisions generated perplexity, and ignorance of what it was then impossible to know, induced troublesome and expensive litigation, and not unfrequently ruinous responsibility; the mist of doubt enveloped subjects which most emphatically demanded perspicuity, and a criterion capable of instantaneous application.

At length Lord Mansfield, who was in law what Newton was in philosophy, dispelled the gloom, established the foundations of commercial jurisprudence upon the broad base of general justice and individual right: uniformity of decision now became

became prevalent, and what before was uncertainty now became system.

> Now at length
> The sacred influence of light appears,
> And shoots into the bosom of the deep
> A glimmering dawn.

Although the words of the statute of Anne and the intention of the legislature could scarcely have been mistaken, yet questions had been agitated relative to the construction of promissory notes similar to those which had previously occurred relative to inland bills, until, in the case of Heylin *v.* Adamson, Lord Mansfield accurately traced the resemblance between promissory notes and bills of exchange, expounded clearly the very letter and spirit of the statute, explained the cause of former mistakes upon the subject, and set the question at rest for ever.

The foundation once laid, the superstructure became easy, and the law relative

tive to negotiable instruments, to use the words of the late Lord Kenyon, is now framed " to meet the exigencies of an extended commerce, without at the same time destroying the established rules of law."

With respect to the present publication it may perhaps be asked, Why, after so many excellent treatises have been written, should another be offered on the same subject? The answer is, that instead of depreciating, the present will increase the value of these publications to that profession for whom they are calculated. The treatises of Kidd, Bailey, Chitty, Montefiore, and Evans, will suffer nothing from this compendium, which attempts to combine and concentrate the characteristic excellencies of each.

The aim of the author in this Alphabetical Analysis, has been to convey an adequate idea of the law relative to this species of commercial contracts as affected

B   by

by bankruptcy, death, infancy, marriage, &c. and to establish a practical guide capable of almost instantaneous application in every case that can possibly occur. The Author has advanced nothing upon *his own* authority; the principles of the most approved writers, founded upon judicial decisions, constitute the materials of which this work is composed, and its arrangement has been calculated to combine the most accurate and copious information with the utmost facility of reference.

Thus, whilst this little volume may be useful to the profession, considered as a copious index to this branch of the reports, it is intended as a complete compendium to the merchant and man of business, whether in his compting-house *or travelling to any distant part of the country;* and by presenting a digest of adjudged cases relative to the predicament in which he may be placed, may enable him to act with promptitude where legal advice cannot

not be procured, and where delay might be productive of mischief. If to the merchant, the professional man, or the public at large this little volume shall be found of practical utility, the object of the writer will be amply attained.

N. B. [The additions of the American Editor are enclosed in brackets.]

A

ABSCONDING *of the Drawee, Acceptor, or Maker of a negotiable instrument.*—If the drawee, acceptor, or maker cannot be found at the place where such instrument is made payable, or abscond the kingdom before it become due, the holder may consider it as dishonoured, and may bring his action immediately against all the parties who have given it currency, although the time of payment is not yet come. The reason assigned by Lord Mansfield in determining this point was, that what the drawee had undertaken had not been performed, the drawee not having given him the credit which was the ground of the contract. Milford *v.* Mayor, Doug. 55.*

ABSCONDING *of the Drawee or Indorser.*— It has been held at Nisi Prius that the absconding of the drawee or indorser will excuse the ne-

glect

* [The case here cited from Douglas, is, that if a bill is not accepted, an action on the bill will lie immediately against the drawer, although the time of payment be not come.]

glect to advise him. Esp. Ca. N. P. 516.* In the case of Walwyn *v.* St. Quentin, Bos. & Pul. 652. the Court, however, declined giving any opinion upon this point.

ACCEPTANCE is an engagement or undertaking [by which a person, after the *issuing* and before the time of its becoming *due*, binds himself] to pay a bill when it becomes due; it is regularly made by the person upon whom the bill is drawn; it may nevertheless be made by his agent, properly authorised for that purpose. [Or by another for his *honour*, or, supra protest. vid. infra.†]—An acceptance may be given either *verbally* or *in writing*, and it may be considered as *absolute, collateral, conditional,* or *partial.*

ACCEPTANCE *absolute* is an engagement to pay according to the tenor of the bill; it is usually given by writing upon the bill the word *accepted,* [or, *accepts*] with the name or initials of the drawee. The holder of a bill has a right to insist upon a *written* acceptance, which is essentially necessary to give the instrument the full benefit of circulation. In accepting a bill payable *after sight,* it is customary to write also *the day* upon which the acceptance is made.

If the drawee keep the bill a longer time than is usual, or do any other act which, upon a fair construction, gives credit to the instrument, and thereby induces the holder not to protest

---

* [So will the circumstance of his having drawn without having funds in the hands of his drawee. Chitty, 192. et vid. tit. *Notice.*]

† [Any thing written on the bill by the drawee, as " *seen,*" " *presented,*" will, if unexplained by other circumstances, amount to an acceptance. Comb. 40. And see further, as to

protest it as dishonoured, this will amount to an absolute acceptance, as will also an agreement to pay at a future period. See *Agreement, Promise.*

Acceptance *collateral.* See *Acceptance upon honour, or supra protest.*

Acceptance *conditional* is an agreement to pay according to the tenor of the acceptance, as where the party renders himself liable for payment upon a contingency only. Any act which evinces an intention not to be bound unless upon a certain event, will be sufficient to give the acceptance the operation of a conditional one. Conditional acceptances have the same obligatory effect as absolute acceptances, and become absolute as soon as the contingency happens, or the condition is performed. When a conditional acceptance is made in *writing* the party making it should also *express the annexed condition,* otherwise he will not be enabled to avail himself of such condition against any other subsequent party; and it is incumbent upon such acceptor to prove the condition. Mason *v.* Hunt, Doug. 296.

Whether there has been an absolute or conditional acceptance, or the extent of a condition,

what will be considered equivalent to an acceptance, 1 Bull. N. P. 270. 1 Atk. 71. 1 T. R. 269. Beawes 466. 3 Burr. 1663. 2 Str. 955.]

dition, is a question of construction, always depending upon the particular circumstances of the individual case; but whether an acceptance is *absolute* or *conditional* is for the decision of the Court, and not the Jury. Per Buller, 1 T. R. 186.

Acceptance *partial* is an agreement to pay according to the tenor of the acceptance, and may vary with respect to *sum, time,* or *place:* it may also vary from the tenor, in the manner in which the acceptor undertakes to pay the bill. All these acceptances, although the holder of the bill may refuse each, will nevertheless bind the acceptor; and the holder of the bill, in either of these cases, if he mean to have recourse to the other parties in default of payment, should give notice to all of them of such acceptance, and express in such notice the nature of it; for any act from whence it can be collected that he does not acquiesce in the acceptance, such as a general notice of non-acceptance, will be a waiver of it. 1 T. R. 182. See *Waiver.**

Acceptance *upon Honour,* or, as it is usually termed, *supra protest,* is a collateral acceptance, and may be made where the drawee refuses to accept,

* [1 Str. 214. 1152. 1195. 1212. Mar. 21. 11 Mod. 190. Beawes 481. Bull. N. P. 270. 2 Wils. 9. 1 T. R. 182. Cowp. 571.]

accept, and some third person, after protest for non-acceptance, accepts for the honour of the bill, the drawer, or any particular indorser; in which latter case he should immediately send the protest to the indorser, because the person making such protest is stiled the *acceptor for the honour* of the person in whose behalf he comes forward, in which case he acquires certain rights, and subjects himself to the same obligations as if the bill had been originally directed to him.

ACCEPTANCE *upon Honour, by whom it may be given.*—Not only a stranger, but the drawee may accept a bill for the honour of the drawer, or any of the indorsers. The difference between such a partial and general acceptance is, that, in the latter case, he renders himself primarily liable, and the general acceptance is presumptive evidence of his possessing sufficient effects; whereas, by accepting specially, though liable to the demands of the holder as if the acceptance were general, he only engages as a surety for the particular person on whose behalf he comes forward, and is entitled to an indemnity from the person, or any of the antecedent parties.

Acceptance

Acceptance upon Honour after the time appointed for payment, if made to pay according to the tenor, will be considered as a general acceptance to pay on demand. Jackson *v.* Piggott, Ld. Raym. 364; Salk. 127. Carth. 459.

It has been said, that if the holder be dissatisfied with the acceptance *supra protest*, and insist upon a simple acceptance, and protest the bill for want of it, the acceptor should renounce the acceptance he has made, and should insist that it be cancelled, otherwise he acts imprudently. Beawes' Pl. 37.

A bill previously accepted *supra protest*, may be accepted by some other individual *supra protest* also, in honour of some particular person. Beawes' Pl. 42.

It appears doubtful whether the possessor of a bill is bound to receive an acceptance *supra protest*, if offered by a responsible person. Beawes is of opinion that he is bound; whilst by others it is held, that the holder need not acquiesce in any case. 12 Mod. 410. *et vi.* Beawes' Pl. 37.

Mode of accepting upon Honour, or supra protest.——The acceptor must in this case appear personally before a notary public, accompanied by

two

two witnesses, and declare that he accepts such protested bill in honour of the drawer or indorser, and that he will satisfy the same at the time limited: he must afterwards subscribe the bill with his own hand thus; " Accepted supra protest in honour of A. B.;" or, as is more usual, " Accepts S. T."

An acceptance supra protest may be so worded, that though it be intended for the honour of the drawer, yet it may equally bind the indorser; but in this case it must be sent to the latter. Beawes' Pl. 38. 457.

Mr. Evans, in a late and excellent Essay on Bills of Exchange (published by Mr. Kearsley in Fleet-street,) observes, that English writers have fallen into mistakes on the subject of acceptance supra protest, by adopting and incorporating into the English law the principles of foreign jurists founded upon foreign laws. The existence of such a collateral engagement, Mr. Evans observes, is a matter of perfect familiarity, that whoever first stated this maxim as part of English jurisprudence fell into the error of adopting as a general principle of mercantile law an institution founded upon the positive laws of other countries. Mr. Evans,

Evans, whose inferences appear to be conclu-
sive upon this point observes, that, by the
law of France, a protest was essentially necessary to enable the holder to maintain his action
against the drawer, and cites from Pothier,
that "in order to subject the drawer, or indorsers to an action *negotiorum gestorum* at the
suit of the person discharging such bill for
their honour, such bill must be protested by
the bearer. The reason is, that as the drawer
and indorsers only become debtors upon the
bill in consequence of the protest, it is necessary that such protest should be made before he
can allege that he has acquitted them from
that debt, and consequently before he can be
entitled to maintain the action *negotiorum gestorum* against them." By the law of England,
however, it is well known that a protest of an
inland bill is not necessary, except with regard
to damages and interest; the reason, therefore,
of the foreign law is inapplicable, and there is
no positive law existing on the subject. In
case of a foreign bill, however, the protest forms
an essential part of the custom of merchants; to
foreign bills therefore, the law which by other
writers has been stated generally, may be cor-
rectly

rectly but exclusively applied. Evans on bills, p. 34.

ACCEPTANCE *verbal.*—A verbal acceptance is equally binding upon the drawee as a written one. Holt, 297.

The words, "leave the bill and I will accept it," will amount to a complete and absolute acceptance, although the drawee had no consideration for the promise. Burr. 1669.—See *Agreement, Promise.*

ACCEPTANCE, *what will amount to one.*—This is a question of construction to be decided by a Jury, but it may be inferred that any act of the drawee evincing his consent to comply with the request of the drawer; such as the words, "seen"—"presented"—"the day of the month," or a direction to a third person to pay the bill, will amount to an acceptance. Vin. Ab. tit. bills of Exch. I. 4. Comb. 401; Moor *v.* Whitby, Bull. N. P. 270; Burn. 1669; Poth's Pl. 45.

If the drawee return the bill, having written any thing upon it (as the day on which it will become due), this, unless explained by other circumstances, will constitute an acceptance. But it has been decided in the case of Powell

C   *v.* Mon-

v. Monnier, 1 Atk. 611, that where a drawee kept a bill for some days without objection, and whilst he had it in his possession made an entry of it in his bill-book (according to his usual practice) under a particular number, and wrote *upon the bill* the same number, with the day on which it would become due, and afterwards sent it back, refusing to accept it, the Court seemed to be of opinion that these circumstances alone did not amount to an acceptance.

It was laid down by Lord Mansfield, in the case of Pierson *v.* Dunlop, that the mere answer of a merchant to the drawer of a bill, saying that he will duly honour it, is no acceptance, unless accompanied with circumstances which may induce a third person to take the bill by indorsement; but if there are any such circumstances, it may amount to an acceptance, though the answer be contained in a letter to the drawer.

If upon presentment the drawee *promise* to accept at any future period such bills as may be drawn hereafter, although no such bill were made at the time of the promise, or do any other act accrediting the bill, which induces the

the holder not to protest it, this will amount to a complete and absolute acceptance: but it has been adjudged, that if the drawee say to the holder, upon his application for acceptance, " there is your bill, it is all right;" or, "leave the bill and I will examine into it," (although in the latter case the bill was left eight or ten days, and being then called for, the drawee offered to let the holder sell some effects, and pay himself,) this will not amount to an acceptance. Bayl. 48; Peach *v.* Kay, Esp. 17. Rep. temp. Hardwicke.

In those cases, however, where the undertaking is doubtful, the drawee will be at liberty to prove some circumstance which does away the presumption. Powell *v.* Monnier, 1 Atk. 611.

ACCEPTANCE, *when to be made.* It has been said that the bill should be left with the drawee *twenty-four hours,* that the drawee may look into his accounts and determine whether he will accept or not; but a bill or note must not be left on a presentment for payment, Ld. Raym. 281. Str. 550. Leaving the bill, however, although customary, Mr. Evans says, is nevertheless not demandable of right, the

law

law in no case compelling a man to part with his security.

ACCEPTANCE *after forged Indorsement.* See *Forgery.*

ACCEPTANCE, *payable at a banker's discharged by neglect in presentment.* See *Discharge.*

ACCEPTANCE, *what it admits in evidence.* An acceptance admits the ability of the drawer to make the bill, and, if made *after sight*, his signature. Wilkinson *v.* Lutwidge, Str. 648; Jenyns *v.* Fowler, Str. 946; but an acceptance though made after sight of an indorsement, does not admit the ability or signature of the indorser. Smith *v.* Chester, 1 T. R. 654; 7 T. R. 604, 612. See *Evidence, Signature.*

ACCEPTANCE *of a Bill,* or giving a promissory note, how far á good payment of an antecedent debt, see *Payment.*

ACCEPTANCE, *its general obligation.* As the interests of *third persons* are generally involved in the efficacy of a bill, an acceptance when the bill is in the hands of a third person, will bind the drawee although he received no consideration for it, and even although that very circumstance was known to the holder. 3 & 4 T. R. 183, 339; and upon this principle

it

it has been decided, that an executor giving his acceptance on account of debts due from his testator, has by such act admitted assets, and thereby made himself personally responsible, although there should be no effects. 1 T. R. 487. The obligation of an acceptance is irrevocable, and cannot be in general discharged by any other act than payment by the acceptor, or by some other person. 1 H. Bl. 88; Poth's Pl. 76. 118.—An absolute acceptance may nevertheless in particular cases be waived. See *Waiver of Acceptance, Discharge, Liability, Presentment.*

ACCEPTOR is that party who agrees, either verbally, in writing, or constructively from his conduct, to pay the bill. Previous to such acceptance he is called *the drawee.*

No action, generally speaking, can be brought against an acceptor *after payment of the bill,* although such bill be afterwards indorsed, the contract between the parties being terminated by payment, and the subsequent indorsement being valid only against the person making it. 1 H. B. 89.

The contract of the acceptor being absolute, he cannot in general insist, as a defence, on

the

the want of presentment of the bill at the precise time when due, or an indulgence to any of
the other parties, Esp. N. P. 46: and it appears to have been decided, that the acceptor
cannot insist, as a defence in an action, upon
the want of a presentment before the commencement of it. Bayl. 78, *n. b.* 108, *n. a.*

In case of a foreign bill, where the course
of exchange has altered, the acceptor will only
be obliged to pay according to the rate of such
exchange when the bill became due. Poth.
Pl. 174. See *Exchange.*

ACCEPTOR, *in what case he may insist on the
want of presentment.*—If he undertake, by his
acceptance, to pay within a certain time *after
demand*, he may insist upon the want of presentment, 2 Show. 235: and it is said where
he appoints the payment to be made by another person, as at his banker's, not only he, but
every other person is, *prima facie*, entitled to
insist upon the want of a proper presentment
to such person; but this point is doubtful.
Stra. 1195; Bayl. 78. acc. Smith *v.* de la Fon-
taine, Bayl. 78, *n. a.* ant.—Such *prima facie*
evidence may, however, be rebutted by proof
of the want of effects in the hands of such
banker. Bayl. 78.

ACCEPTOR,

ACCEPTOR, *his liability with respect to costs.* If the holder of a dishonoured bill sues all the parties to it at the same time, the acceptor is the only person responsible to the plaintiff for the costs of all the actions. Smith v. Woodcock. Same v. Dudley, 4 T. R. 691.

ACCEPTOR, *what must be proved in an action against him.*—The plaintiff must prove the acceptance or signature of the defendant, and the necessary Indorsements; and in the former case, the signature of the drawer, if the acceptance was made without sight of the bill; and if the bill was accepted by an agent or servant, he must prove that such agent or servant was legally authorised by his principal.*

ACCEPTOR *of an accommodation bill,* if obliged to pay such bill, may sue the drawer, upon his implied contract to indemnify him.

ACCEPTOR, *if becoming bankrupt,* see *Bankruptcy.*

ACCEPTOR, *how far responsible in case of a forged bill.* If a person accept a bill which is actually *shewn to him,* he is answerable, although the name of the drawer should be forged, because his engagement has relation to that individual writing; but if *without seeing the instrument* he engages to pay a bill of a certain

* [In a case in Sayer, 223. the court suffered the jury to determine whether, the acceptance of the bill when the names of all the indorsers were upon it, together with the promise of the defendant to pay it, did not amount to an *admission,* that the name of every indorser was of his hand-writing. This report cannot be relied upon, because it is in direct opposition to numerous and positive decisions, in all which it is uniformly laid down that the hand-writing of the first indorser must be proved in an action against the acceptor, notwithstanding such indorsement was on the bill at the time it was accepted. 1 T. R. 654. 3 T. R. 174. 182. 481. 1 H. Bl. Rep. C. B. 569.]

tain tenor drawn by a particular person, such engagement only refers to a bill actually drawn by the person mentioned, and consequently the acceptor in this case will not be liable.

ACCEPTORS *several, what must be proved in an action against them.* The signature and acceptance of each must be in this case proved, Esp. Ca. N. P. 135, or that a partnership existed, and that an acceptance was made by one of them for himself and partners, Peake, 16. See *Partners, Evidence.*

ACCEPTOR, *how far discharged if taken in execution.* See *Discharge, Execution.*

ACCEPTOR *upon Honour, what must be done to entitle him to his action of indemnity.* An acceptor upon honour, is bound, in order to maintain his action for an indemnity, to give immediate notice to the person on whose behalf he engages, and such notice will be sufficient; and it is stated by Pothier, that the drawer or indorser is entitled to the same *objections* in an action brought by the person accepting for his honour, as upon an action in chief; otherwise the person whose business is undertaken would be in a worse condition than if it had not been so undertaken, which the na-

ture

ture of the implied contract of *negotiorum ges-torum* does not admit. Evans, p. 37.

ACCIDENT.—In case of the loss of an accepted bill, notice should be immediately given; for it is said, that such loss will be no excuse for not giving regular notice. Poth. Pl. 125. See *Loss, Notice.*

ACCOMMODATION Bill or Note.— Where any party accepts a bill or note without any consideration, but merely for accommodation only, payment of part of such bill or note will not discharge the drawer. Cooke's Bank. L. 167.: but if the holder of an accommodation bill receive part from the drawer, and take a promise from him upon the back of the bill for payment of the remainder at an enlarged time, it may become doubtful how far such act will discharge the acceptor. It ought to be left to a jury to say whether this is not a waiver of the acceptance; but it ought to be left to them with strong observations to shew that it is. Bayley, 55; Ellis *v.* Galindo, B. R. M. 24 G. 3. cited Doug. 250, *n.*

Accommodation Bill, *what must be proved by the Acceptor of one in an action against the Drawer.* If the acceptor of an accommodation

tion bill sue the drawer, he must prove the hand-writing of the defendant and payment by himself, or something equivalent, such as his being in prison, or a capias ad satisfaciendum.

ACT of BANKRUPTCY.—If a man become a bankrupt, all his property is, by the assignment of the commissioners to the assignees, vested in the assignees by relation to the act of bankruptcy, so as to defeat all intermediate acts done by such bankrupt to dispose of his property; and consequently the right of transfer, from the time of the act of bankruptcy, is in the assignees. Beawes, 469; 2 H. B. 335; Peake, 50. See *Bankrupt, Bankruptcy, Dividend, Proof.*

ACT of BANKRUPTCY. If the acceptor of a bill or maker of a note absent himself to the holder upon *the morning* when such bill becomes due, this has been held to amount to an act of bankruptcy, cited by Mr. Justice Buller in the case of Leftly *v.* Mills, Evans, 46.

ACTION *against the Drawer, when it may be brought.*—If the drawee of a bill of exchange should not accept such bill when duly presented for the purpose of acceptance, the drawer will be responsible, whether such bill

were

were drawn on his account or that of a third person; and an action may be commenced against him immediately, *before the time specified in the bill*, not only for the principal sum, but also in certain cases for damages and interest, as a consequence of the bill's not being honoured. 2 H. B. 379; Poth. Pl. 62.

ACTION, *in case of non-acceptance, by and against whom to be brought.*——The action may be brought not only against the drawee, but against all the antecedent indorsers, the debt being by law supposed to be contracted at the time the bill is drawn. Milford *v.* Mayor, Doug. 54; Bull. N. P. 269: and it may be brought by the drawer or indorser, not legally bound to pay, in consequence of the neglect of the holder in giving due notice for non-acceptance for the money so paid, through misrepresentation, mistake, or ignorance of the fact. Chatfield *v.* Paxton and Co. Sit. after Tr. T. 38 Geo. 3. cited by Chitty, 103.

ACTION *against the indorser* may be commenced without making any previous demand of the drawer.

ACTION *by drawer against acceptor after payment by the drawer.* For what must be proved in such action, see *Evidence.*

ACTION,

ACTION, *in what cases maintainable.* An action may be brought upon a mere transfer by delivery upon a bill so transferable, if made on account of a pre-existing debt, or for a valuable consideration, passing to the assignee at the time of the assignment, as where goods are sold to him. 6 T. R. 52; 7 T. R. 64.: unless it were agreed expressly at the time of the transfer, that the assignee should take the instrument assigned as payment, and run the risk of its being paid, on the consideration of such transfer. 7 T. R. 65, 66; Holt, 121. See *Payment.*

ACTION, *by whom maintainable upon bills transferable by delivery.* The assignee's name not being upon the instrument, and there being no privity of contract between him and any assignee bearing such after-assignment by himself, no person but his *immediate* assignee can maintain an action against him. Ld. Raym. 928.: neither can action be brought upon transfer by delivery made without indorsement, merely by way of sale of the bill, as in the course of a discount. 3 T. R. 757; Esp. Ca. N. P. 447: nor where the assignee expressly agrees to take it in payment and run all risks,

has

has he any right of action, if such bill should eventually prove of no value: but where a bill is assigned for a good consideration by a person knowing it to be of no value, he would in all cases be compellable to refund the money received. 12 Mod. 517; 3 T. R. 759. Holt, 121.

ACTION, *in case of loss or robbery.* If an instrument, transferable by mere delivery, get into the hands of any person not aware of such loss or robbery, having paid a good consideration for the same previous to its becoming due, notwithstanding such person derived his interest from the person who found or stole it, the original holder who lost it will forfeit all right of action. Good *v.* Coe, cited 7 T. R. 427. See *Loss, Robbery.*

ACTION *upon payment upon honour or supra protest.* Although with respect to other debts a *Stranger* not having any interest therein, does not entitle himself to the rights of a creditor, unless he have the consent of the creditor or debtor to such payment; yet with regard to a bill of exchange, a stranger paying such instrument supra protest, acquires the same rights as the proprietor of the bill had, although no

regular

regular transfer were made to him, and may maintain an action against the person who discharged the bill, either on the instrument itself, or on the count for money paid to the defendant's use. Esp. N. P. 112; Poth. Pl. 171; Lutw. 891; 1 T. R. See *Acceptance upon Honour or Supra Protest.*

ACTION *usually brought upon bills or notes.* Although *an action of debt* will lay as the sum to be recovered is specific, yet the most extensive remedy upon bills, checks, or notes, (and indeed the only one where no privity of contract exists between the parties, as between the indorsee and acceptor of a bill, and the maker of a note,) is the *action of assumpsit;* and this action is maintainable against *all* the parties wherever a liability is imposed, or legal rights created: thus it may be brought by the holder, payee, indorsee, &c. of a bill or note against the acceptor, drawer, or maker, or all the antecedent parties.

ACTION, *in what cases not maintainable.* No action can be maintained (unless under special circumstances, to be shewn on the record) against a person who becomes a party to the bill subsequent to the holder; nor can a plain-

tiff

tiff maintain his action against the person from whom he received a bill or note, unless he gave him a valuable consideration for it. 7 T. R. 350, 571; 1 Lutw. 886; 10 Mod. 36; 1 Wils. 185; 4 Bro. P. C. 604.

Where a bill is returned upon the drawer for non-payment, he cannot afterwards negotiate it so as to charge the acceptor with an action on the bill at the suit of the indorsee. Beck *v.* Robley, 1 H. B. 1589.

ACTION, *how extinguished.* If the holder of a bill make the acceptor his executor, the right of action against all the parties to the bill is by this action extinguished. Poth's Pl. 191; 1 Rol. Abr. 922; Plowd. 184, 543; Salk. 299; 2 Bl. Com. 511, 512; 3 Bl. Com. 18.

ACTION *against some of the parties will not preclude a remedy against the others.*—The party entitled to such remedy may bring his action either severally against each of the parties to the instrument, or collectively against all; and an action commenced against any one of them will not preclude any other remedy against the rest; but satisfaction by any one will discharge all the rest. Poth. Pl. 160; Hull *v.* Pitfield, 1 Wils. 46. See *Declaration, Evidence, Execution, Judgment, Remedy.*

ACTION

ACTION OF DEBT. See *Debt.*

ADMINISTRATOR. See *Executor.*

ADVICE. In cases where the drawee of a bill of exchange is to expect further instructions relative to its payment, it is usual to insert the words, *as per advice:* where no further instructions are to be transmitted, acceptance or payment is ordered *without further advice,* and generally neither of these words are inserted. In the former case the drawee, it is said, may not pay without further advice; in the latter case, he may. Poth. Pl. 36, 169. This, however true with respect to other countries, as between the person advising and his correspondent or agent, is nevertheless inapplicable in this. By the laws of England, if a bill be refused acceptance or payment, the bill is considered as dishonoured, and the holder may proceed accordingly.

AGENT.—It is a general principle in law, that whenever a man has a power as owner to do a thing, he may, as consistent with this right, do it by deputy, whether such person be an attorney, agent, factor, or servant. Hence it follows, that any person may draw, accept, or indorse bills by his agent as well as

by

by himself. In these cases he is said to draw,
indorse, or accept bills by procuration. Beawes'
Pl. 83.

AGENT, *who may act as such.*—This being
an office merely ministerial, *infants, married
women, persons attainted, excommunicated,* or
outlawed, and others incapable of binding themselves in their *own right* by contract, may be
agents for the above purposes. Co. Lit. 52.

AGENT, *how appointed.*—It has been asserted
that agents should be appointed by a formal
power of attorney, Beawes' Pl. 86. Marius,
2d edit. p. 104: but this is not necessary, for
the authority of an agent to draw, indorse and
accept bills in the name of his principal, is
usually by parol. Chitty cites 7 T. R. 209;
12 Mod. 564.

AGENT, *how far he can bind his principal.*—If
a person be appointed a general agent, as in the
case of a factor for a merchant resident abroad,
the principal is bound by all his acts; but an
agent *specially* appointed under a restrictive and
circumscribed power, cannot bind his principal
by any act whereby he exceeds his authority.
The following authorities are cited in corrobo-
ration of this doctrine. Fenn *v.* Harrison,

D 2   3 T. R.

3 T. R. 757; Esp. Ca. N. P. The case of Nixon v. Bromham, Sel. Ca. 17. seems, however, to contradict the principle. Chitty on Bills.

In a case where A. desired B. to get a bill discounted for him, but declared that he would not indorse, the majority of the court decided, that no representation of B. could bind A. as an indorser, though it was insisted that what B. had done was within the scope of his employment, which was, to raise money on the bill. Upon a second trial, however, it appearing that A. did not declare that he would not indorse, it was adjudged, that as he had authorised B. to get the bill discounted without restraining his authority as to the mode of doing it, he was bound by his acts. Chitty, p. 25, cites 3 T. R. 757; 4 T. R. 177; Collis v. Emmet, H. B. 313; Russel v. Langstaff, Dougl. 514.

AGENT, *what will amount to a general authority*. See *Authority*.

AGENT, *acting upon implied authority.*—If an agent has upon a former occasion, in the absence of his principal, usually accepted his bills, and such principal has, upon his return, approved thereof, the acceptance of such agent would

would bind him in a second absence from
home. A *subsequent assent* of the principal
will also make the act of the agent binding.

AGENT, *general*, although exceeding his authority, will nevertheless bind his principal in
every act he does: it therefore is incumbent
upon his employer to take very particular care
whom he authorises to execute such an important trust. And since a master, who has
empowered his servant to draw bills of exchange in his name, is bound by all acts of the
servant subsequent to such servant's leaving his
service, unless due notice be given, it is incumbent upon the employer to give notice to
all his correspondents *individually, notice in the
Gazette not being sufficient, unless brought home
to the person insisting on the want of it.* 9 Ca. 75;
Rol. Ab. 330.

AGENT, *how he is to execute his functions.*—
In executing the authority entrusted to him,
the agent must, as in all other acts, do it *in the
name and on the account* of his principal,
otherwise the latter will not be bound, and the
agent will be personally responsible. 9 Co. 75;
1 Sto. 705; Com. Dig. tit. Attorney, c. 14;
Beawes' Pl. 83, 84, 85, 86, 87; 6 T. R. 176,
177;

177; Stra. 955; 1 T. R. 181; Rep. temp. H. 3. *contra*, cited by Chitty, p. 27.

An agent cannot delegate his authority, unless an express authority be given him for that purpose. 9 Co. 75; Rol. Ab. 330; Bunb. 166.

AGENT, *his duty on presenting bills for acceptance.*—Bills for acceptance should be presented by an agent as soon as possible, because by acceptance only, the drawee of the bill becomes debtor, and responsible to the holder; and it is laid down by foreign jurists, Pothier and Marius, that if the affairs of the drawee should be deranged, an agent, having neglected to present the bill for acceptance, would be responsible in damages and interest to his employer.

AGENT, *manner in which he should accept, draw, and indorse bills.*—In these cases it is incumbent upon the agent, if required, to produce his authority, or in the alternative, the holder, it is said, may consider the bill as dishonoured, and act accordingly. Beawes' Pl. 87.

Mr. Chitty expresses some doubt whether the holder of a bill would be in any case bound to acquiesce in the acceptance by agent, because

it

it multiplies the proof which he will be obliged to produce if compelled to bring an action on the bill. Esp. Cas. Ni. Pri. 115, 269. With due deference, however, to the observation of this gentleman it may be observed, that it is a principle of law that what a man may do individually he may do by deputy, and mercantile transactions and commercial intercourse being founded upon reciprocal facilities, innumerable impediments would arise if objections which may be termed *apices juris* should be suffered to prevent that, which in many instances must, if at all, be performed by agency, and what in the mercantile world is usually transacted through the medium of correspondents or agents. It does not appear that this point ever became the subject of litigation, if it did, there is little doubt but a jury composed of English merchants would decide the question in the affirmative. See *Authority*.

AGREEMENT, *in what case a waiver of acceptance.* An agreement to consider the acceptance at an end, or a message to the acceptor upon an accommodation bill, that the business has been settled with the drawer, and that he need give himself no further trouble, have

have been adjudged to amount to a waiver of an absolute acceptance. Walpole *v.* Pulteney, cited Doug. 247; Black *v.* Peele, cited ib. See *Waiver*.

AGREEMENT, *how far a discharge of acceptance*. An agreement entered into by the holder of a bill of exchange not to sue the acceptor, upon his making affidavit that the acceptance is a forgery; and if such affidavit be made and sworn accordingly, he cannot afterwards bring an action upon such bill, although the affidavit should be false. Peake, 187; Esp. Ca. N. P. 178.

An agreement to receive the bill of lading from the acceptor which was the consideration of the acceptance, in a case where the bill was accepted in consideration of the future consignment of goods to the acceptor, and the prospect of the commission on the sale thereof, and the holder of the bill knowing the nature of the acceptance, receives the bill of lading, &c. in pursuance of the agreement; the acceptor, by this act of the holder, will be discharged from his acceptance. Mason *v.* Hunt, Doug. 298. See *Discharge*.

AGREEMENT *to accept, how far obligatory*. See *Promise to accept*.

AGREEMENT

AGREEMENT *to take bills or notes in payment, how far operative.* See *Payment.*

ALTERATION, *before Acceptance or In-dorsement.*—If the bill or note, whilst in the hands of the payee, or any other holder, be altered in any material instance, as in date, sum, &c. without consent of the drawee, he will be discharged from his liability, although such bill or note may afterwards come into the hands of an indorsee not aware of the altera-tion: but in this case, if altered before accept-ance or indorsement, the acceptor or indorser can take no advantage of the alteration. Mar. 138, 140; Beawes' Pl. 194; and the consent of any one of the parties to the alteration will in general estop him from taking an advantage of it. 4 T. R. 320.

ALTERATION *of a Bill.* It was decided in the case of Master *v.* Miller, by the opinion of all the Judges except Mr. Justice Buller, that any alteration of a bill after it has been issued will entirely destroy the obligation. In this particular case the date of a bill payable at three months after date was altered, after ac-ceptance, from the 26th to the 20th of March; it did not appear by whom this alteration was made,

made, but it was resolved that the acceptor was not liable to pay the amount to a fair holder, and the obligation of the instrument was utterly destroyed.

ALTERATION *of a Bill, its operation with respect to the Stamp.* If a bill be made with a proper stamp, and afterwards altered by the consent of the parties, though before negotiation, a new stamp is necessary, as it is a different contract, Wilson *v.* Justice, Sit. after Mich. T. 1796. Bowman *v.* Nichol, 5 T. R. 537.

ALTERATION *of an Acceptance, how far it will discharge the Acceptor.* If the holder of a bill alter a partial into a general acceptance, this will not be a waiver or discharge of the acceptor's liability under his partial acceptance. Price *v.* Shute, Beawes' Pl. 222; Molloy's Pl. 28; 4 T. R. 336, cited by Chitty, p. 85.

ARREST, *legality of a second under same writ.*—In a case where defendant was arrested, and discharged out of custody upon giving the plaintiff a draft for part of the money due, on which he was discharged out of custody; but the draft having been dishonoured, he was retaken upon the same writ, and it was held that

that this proceeding was perfectly warrantable and regular. Lord Kenyon observed upon this occasion, "that if the bill which is given in payment does not turn out to be productive, it is not that which it purports to be, and which the party receiving it expects it to be, and therefore he may consider it as a nullity, and act as if no such bill had been given." 6 T. R. 52.

ARREST, *when illegal.*—By 38 Geo. 3. c. 1. s. 8, no person shall be held to bail, unless the affidavit of the debt allege, that no offer has been made to pay the debt in bank notes payable on demand. See *Tender.*

ASSETS are those effects of a deceased person in the hands of his representative, whether as executor or administrator, and they are to be applied to payment of the debts of the deceased according to the nature and legal *priority* of such debts.

ASSETS, *if deficient, in what case the executor is personally responsible.* An acceptance by an executor on account of debts due from his testator, is an admission of assets, and will therefore make him personally responsible if there should be eventually no effects in his hands belonging to his testator. 1 H. B. 622;

E   3 Wils.

3 Wils. 1; 2 Stra. 1260; 2 Barnes, 137;
2 Burr. 1225; 1 T. R. 487. See *Executor.*

ASSIGNEE *of a bankrupt* cannot insist
upon the want of notice of a bill being dishonoured, if the drawer or indorser is a bankrupt
at the time of the acceptance. Esp. Ca. N. P.
516, *sed qu?* See *Bankrupt, Bankruptcy, Dividend, Notice, Proof.*   .

ASSUMPSIT is the species of action ap-
propriated to recover damages upon simple
contract debts, as contra-distinguished from
debt upon specialties. In any case, therefore,
where the law implies a *promise*, this action may
be brought; such as for goods sold and delivered, money had and received, money paid,
laid out and expended, work and labour, &c.
It is usually brought where the damages are
uncertain, in contra-distinction to debt where
the sum is liquidated.

ATTESTATION, in the case of bills under
five pounds, pursuant to 17 Geo. 3. c. 30. s. 1,
must be made by one subscribing witness, and
the indorsement of such bill must also be made
in a similar manner. See *Small Notes, Witnesses,* and *Abstract of this Act in the Appendix.*

AUTHORITY is either *general* or *special,*
and

and may not only be express but implied; and
an authority may be given by parol as well as
in writing. 12 Mod. 564.

AUTHORITY, *the powers conferred by it in
certain cases.* A person signing or indorsing his name on a blank unstamped paper, and
delivering it to another, authorizes such person to insert any sum which that stamp will
warrant in its amount, 1 H. B. 313; Russel *v.*
Langstaffe, Doug. 514: and a letter of attorney, given by an executor to another person,
enabling him to transact the affairs of the
testator in the name of the executor, as executor, and to pay, discharge, and satisfy all
debts due from the testator, will convey sufficient authority to such person to accept a
bill of exchange, in the name of the executor, drawn by a creditor, for the amount of a
debt due from the testator, and make the executor personally liable. Chitty, 25, cites
2 H. B. 618, *sed quære?* 6 T. R. 591, and
1 H. B. 155.

AUTHORITY *of a servant*, signing a bill
must be proved. See *Evidence, Signature.*

AUTHORITY *general, what is evidence of.*
Usual employ is evidence of this, and it is supposed

posed to continue until its determination is *notorious*. 10 Mod. 110; 12 Mod. 346. See *Notice*.

Subsequent assent is evidence of precedent authority. Comb. 450. See *Agent, Evidence.*

B

BAIL, *upon whose account to be considered as holders of a bill.* The bail of the parties sued upon a bill of exchange, or any other persons who on account of any of the parties may have paid the bill, are considered as the holders of the bill, which they hold as a transfer from the person on whose account they have made the payment, and not as upon a transfer from the person they have paid. Hall *v.* Pitfield, B. R. H. T. 17 G. 2.

BALANCE *only proveable under a commission in case of mutual debts.* In case of mutual debts the balance *only* is to be proved under a commission against the acceptor or indorser of a bill or note dishonoured; a debtor of the bank-

E 2   rupt

rupt may therefore set off a bill or note which he holds against him, and is not compellable to pay the whole sum where he is a debtor, and take a dividend as creditor. But this mutuality must exist at the time of the act of bankruptcy. See *Bankruptcy, Dividend, Proof, Set Off.*

BANK NOTES, *their origin, form, &c.*— These instruments derive their origin from the 5th William & Mary, c. 20. s. 19, 20, and the 8 & 9 W. 3. c. 20. s. 30.—The former of these statutes empowered the king to incorporate the persons subscribing towards raising and paying into the receipt of the Exchequer, the sum of 1,200,000*l.* by the name and title of " the Governor and Company of the Bank of England." These notes are made payable *on demand,* and are treated *as money* in the ordinary course of business, and upon payment of them a receipt is given as *for cash.* If they are lost, the true owner may bring an action of trover to recover them: but it has been adjudged that an action for money had and received will not lie against the finder to recover their value, unless money has been actually received for them. Noyes *v.* Price,

An.

An. Sittings London, Hil. T. 16 G. 3; 3 T. R. 554. *Bank notes are not a legal tender if specially objected to on that account at the time of the offer*, although after such tender a creditor cannot arrest his debtor; for by 38 G. 3. c. 1. s. 8, no person shall be held to bail, unless the affidavit of the debt allege, that no offer has been made to pay the debt in bank notes payable on demand.

BANKERS' NOTES, or as they were formerly termed goldsmiths' notes, are promissory notes given by bankers who were originally goldsmiths—they were originally given by bankers to their customers as an acknowledgment for having received money to their use, Holt, 119; 1 Salk. 283. These notes are seldom issued except by country bankers, the use of them being now supplied in the metropolis by checks.—Their form is similar to common promissory notes payable to bearer on demand, and are so stated in pleading. These notes, when issued by London bankers, are called *shop notes*, and whether payable to order or bearer are considered as cash, on account of their being payable *on demand;* like bankers' checks they are generally transferred by delivery: they may notwithstanding be negotiated by

by indorsement, in which case the act of indorsing will make them similar to bills of exchange, and they may be declared upon as such
against the indorser. Love, 58; Ld. Raym. 743;
1 Salk. 132, 3; 4 T. R. 149.

BANKERS' CHECKS, see *Checks*.

BANKRUPT, *payments made by him.*—By 19
G. 2. c. 32, no person shall be liable to refund
any money which *before* the suing out a commission of bankruptcy, was really and *bona
fide*, and in the usual and ordinary course of
trade and dealing received by such person of
any such bankrupt, before such time as the
person receiving the same shall *know, under-
stand*, or *have notice* that he is become a bankrupt; but although *payment by* a bankrupt to
a person not having notice of the bankruptcy
and being a *bona fide* creditor for *goods sold*, or
by the bankrupt's having *drawn, negotiated*, or
accepted a bill of exchange in the usual or ordinary course of trade and dealing, is protected by
the act above cited; yet this statute has been so
strictly construed according to the letter, that
*money paid by a trader after a secret act of bank-
ruptcy* to a *carrier for the carriage of goods* may
be

be recovered back in an action of assumpsit by the assignees of the bankrupt. 5 T. R. 197.

BANKRUPT *depositing a bill by way of pledge.* If a bankrupt, *without putting his name to a bill*, deposit it by way of pledge, it must, like any other pledge, be sold for the benefit of the creditor, and he can only be admitted to prove for the residue, and cannot in this case, as *where the name appears on the bill, prove for the full amount*, and receive dividends from all parties until he has received twenty shillings in the pound. Evans, 219.

BANKRUPTCY *of the drawer or indorser when no excuse for want of notice.* It is an inference by Mr. Chitty, from a case before Lord Thurlow entitled Ex parte Smith, 3 Bro. Ch. 1, that where the drawer *or* indorser is a bankrupt at the time of the acceptance or payment refused, it will be unnecessary to give notice to him or his assignee. This decision related merely to the effect of receiving a composition from the acceptor; in that case Lord Thurlow declared he had often decided that the doctrine of notice which held amongst solvent persons did not apply as between bankrupt estates.

From

From this case, Mr. Evans judiciously observes, there does not appear any sufficient reason to dispense with notice to the drawer who is a bankrupt or to his assignees, and still less for dispensing with such notice to the bankrupt indorser, or his assignees, where the drawer remains solvent, because in these cases their right to recover against the solvent parties may be prejudiced by the want of notice. But where *all* the parties are bankrupts, in such case no prejudice can arise. Evans, 91. See *Excuse, Notice.*

BANKRUPTCY *of different parties to bills and notes, how far the holder may prove against all.* Where different parties to bills or notes have become bankrupts the holder it is said may prove the full amount against them all, in the same manner as he may proceed in different actions at law, until he have received a complete satisfaction; but if he has received any part before he proves, the proof can only be for the balance; but it is conceived by Mr. Evans that in general a dividend must be paid to him for the full amount upon the respective proofs, although he is accountable *as a trustee for the surplus.* For more upon this, see *Dividend, Proof.*

BANKRUPTCY *of parties, for whom the indorser merely became surety, how far he may prove upon their respective estates.*

Mr. Cullen, in his late treatise, ascribes the difference and apparent contrariety of decisions, to a difference in the principle of the cases, and states the distinction according to his view of the subject as follows:—" Where a person merely indorses a bill for the purpose of assisting another in raising money, and is therefore *only a surety*, his demand only arises by the actual payment of the money, which being *after the bankruptcy*, cannot be the subject of a proof; but if he have received the bill upon a *real consideration*, either mediate or immediate, there is a debt then subsisting to which his subsequent payment may refer." Vide Brookes *v.* R gers, 1 H. B. 640; Howis *v.* Wiggins, 4 T. R. 714; *ex parte* Brymer, C. B. L. 164; *ex parte* Seddon, cited 7 T. R. 575.

BANKRUPTCY, *what may be proved in case of mutual debts.* In the case of mutual debts the balance only is to be paid; a debtor of the bankrupt therefore may set off a bill or note which he holds against him, and is not compellable to pay the whole where he is a debtor and

and take a dividend as creditor. But this mutuality must exist at the time of the act of bankruptcy, for the state of the bankrupt's effects cannot afterwards be legally charged to the prejudice of the general creditors; and therefore a debtor can only set off bills or notes which he has received previous to the act of bankruptcy, and it is incumbent upon him to give proof of such receipt. Dickenson *v.* Evans, 6 T. R. 57.

BANKRUPTCY *of the drawee will be no ex-cuse for neglect.* The bankruptcy or known insolvency of the drawee of a bill or maker of a note will be no excuse for a neglect in the holder to make presentment, or to give notice if the drawee had assets in his hands at the time the bill was drawn. Doug. 497, 515; 1 T. R. 408. But see *Excuse, Neglect, Notice.*

BANKRUPTCY, *what costs and charges may be proved under a commission.* The costs and charges of protesting bills *before* an act of bankruptcy may be proved; but those which accrued afterwards cannot; nor is the holder of a bill or note entitled to any interest accruing after the date of the commission issued; nor *where the act of bankruptcy is ascertained* to

                               any

any which might have accrued after the bank-ruptcy; notwithstanding this however, the creditor may prove the full sum for which the notes were given, although he have received five per cent. discount. Coke, 173, 181, 182.

BANKRUPTCY, *how far the liability of parties to a bill is affected by it.* The holder of a negotiable instrument is by the 7th G. 1. c. 31, and 5 G. 2. c. 30, entitled to prove it under a commission of bankruptcy, whether such instrument be due or not at the time of such bankruptcy, and he may in all cases prove it *if in possession of it at that time;* and he may either be petitioning creditor in respect to such bill, or prove it under the commission; and even where it is not due he may receive a dividend of the bankrupt's estate, in the same proportions as the other creditors, deducting interest only after the rate of five per cent. for the time the bill has to run; and in such case the bankrupt is discharged from all liability on the instrument in case of obtaining his certificate, as much as if it had been due before the act of bankruptcy. Cooke's Bank. Laws, 159, 136.

BANKRUPTCY. *Accommodation bills, how*

F *proveable*

proveable under a commission. Where a person has put his name to a negotiable instrument for the accommodation of another, and another bill or note delivered to him as a security is in his possession at the time of the bankruptcy, he will be allowed to prove such bill, although the accommodation bill was not paid until after the bankruptcy; but in this case the dividends will be kept back until it appear what damages have been actually sustained, and whether the bankrupt's estate is exonerated by the holder from that payment to which he is himself liable. Cooke's Bank. L. 159. 366; 7 Durnf. & East, 366; Esp. 134.

BANKRUPTCY *of the acceptor. How the holder of a bill may prove if not in possession of it at the time of the bankruptcy.* This point is to be collected not without some difficulty from the several cases which have been determined. When a bill has been drawn *before*, but indorsed *after* the secret act of bankruptcy of the acceptor to another person, it has been decided, that the indorsee, although he cannot set off the amount of the sum payable to any demand on him by the assignees, (the act of 5th Geo. 2, relating only to mutual debts due before the bankruptcy,)

bankruptcy,) he may nevertheless be a petitioning creditor to the amount, or prove it under
the commission. Nor will the circumstance
of an indorsement *after the bill became due,*
make in this case any difference. Cooke's Bank.
Laws, 19, 164.

BANKRUPTCY *of the drawer, how far an
acceptor knowing of this will be justified in
paying his acceptance.* A case has been decided,
that if a person not having notice of the bankruptcy of the drawer, accept a bill drawn upon
him after such bankruptcy, and even although
he has afterwards heard of the bankruptcy, he
will nevertheless be justified in paying his acceptance. 7 Durn. & East, 711.

BANKRUPTCY, *how far supersedable by the
statute of limitations.* Although negotiable instruments above six years' standing may be
proved under a commission (because the debt
still exists, and no person but the acceptor can
avail himself of the statute of limitations); yet
where the bankrupt himself applied to set aside
the commission on the ground that the petitioning creditor's debt was barred by the above
statute, the commission was superseded. 1 T.
R. 405.

BANKRUPTCY

BANKRUPTCY *of a person for whom bills have been discounted.* If the holder in this case prove the aggregate amount of the bills excepting them as a security, and any of the bills are afterwards paid in full, the amount of the bills must be deducted from the proof, and the future dividends must be paid only upon the remainder of the debt. Cooke 119, 120, 155, 156.

BANKRUPT'S CERTIFICATE.—Any bill or note given by a bankrupt as a consideration for signing his certificate or withdrawing a petition against it, is illegal by statute, and such instrument is null and void. See *Considerations illegal.*

BEARER.—If a bill or note be made payable *to bearer* it will pass by delivery only, without indorsement; and whoever fairly acquires a right to it may maintain an action against the drawer or acceptor. If, however, such instrument should be in fact indorsed, the indorser will in this, as in other cases, become chargeable as an original drawer. Bills payable *to bearer* are contra-distinguished to those payable *to order*, which can only be transferred by indorsement and delivery. Bills payable to

fictitious

fictitious payees are to be considered as bills payable to bearer. See *Fictitious Persons*, *Forgery*.

BILLS of EXCHANGE. A bill of exchange is a written order or request, addressed by one person to another, desiring him to pay a certain sum of money at a time therein specified, to a *third person* or to *his order*, or it may be made payable to *bearer*.

In the former case the instrument is negotiable by indorsement; in the latter, by delivery only. The holder of a negotiable instrument originally payable *to bearer*, may nevertheless restrain its general negotiability by a special indorsement; and a special indorsee may by a general indorsement make the instrument payable to bearer.

BILLS OF EXCHANGE, *their origin*. Although writers are considerably divided in opinion with respect to this point, an inference drawn from the 5th Ric. 2. st. 1, 2, appears to warrant the conclusion that foreign bills were introduced into this country previous to the year 1381, and the earliest decision sanctioning this custom of remitting from abroad appears to have been in the case of Oaste *v.*

F 2   Taylor,

Taylor, Cro. Jac. 306; 1 Roll. Abr. 6. Upon the first introduction of these instruments, our courts would only give effect to Bills made between Merchants Strangers and English Merchants; this however was soon extended to all traders, and finally to all persons indiscriminately. Chit. p. 12, 13.

BILLS OF EXCHANGE *how divided.* Bills of exchange are divided into *foreign* and *inland:* the former are those which pass from one country to another, and the latter are transacted by parties all of whom are resident in the same country. Foreign bills are generally drawn in sets, to obviate the dangers of navigation; inland bills are sometimes, but very rarely, drawn in this mode.

By the 9th & 10th Will. III. c. 17, and 3 & 4 Anne, c. 9, all distinctions between foreign and inland bills, as far as respects the custom of Merchants, were removed, and the established law of the country is in most cases applicable to both.

BILLS OF EXCHANGE, *names and liability of the parties.* The person making or drawing the bill is called *the drawer,* the person to whom it is addressed *the drawee;* who, when he has
undertaken

undertaken to pay the amount, is termed *the acceptor.* The person in whose favour the bill is drawn, is called *the payee*, who, if he appoint some other person to receive the money, is then termed *the indorser*, and the person so appointed the *indorsee.* The person who may happen to be in possession of the bill is called *the holder.*

Any persons capable of binding themselves by a contract, may draw or accept a bill of exchange, or be parties to a promissory note, or be in any manner concerned in negotiating either of these instruments. Upon this principle an infant cannot be sued upon a bill of exchange, because he is by law incapable of binding himself upon a contract, nor a married woman, except in certain cases, such as where by the custom of London she has the privilege of trading as a *femme sole*, and of course binding herself by contract. By several modern decisions it has indeed been held, that a married woman may contract so as to bind herself if living apart from her husband, and having a permanent separate maintenance secured to her by deed. 4 T. R. 361, 766; 5 T. R. 604; Esp. Ca. N. P. 6. These cases, however,

ever, and the principle upon which they are founded, have been questioned by the present Lord Chancellor.

BILLS OF EXCHANGE, *how favoured in legal construction*. Bills or notes import a valuable consideration, which it is *not* incumbent upon the holder to prove; and in no case will the defendant be admitted to prove that he received *no consideration*, unless in an action brought against him by the person with whom he was *immediately* concerned in the negotiation of the instrument. 1 Bla. Rep. 445. Bills of exchange, although not specialties, are nevertheless possessed of the same privileges as other bonds or specialties, particularly when in the hands of third persons: and a bill of exchange derives these privileges, not from its form, nor from its being in writing, but to strengthen and facilitate that commercial intercourse between merchants of different countries, which is carried on through the medium of this species of security.

BILLS OF EXCHANGE, *how far operative with respect to persons incapacitated*. Infants, married women, &c. being legally incapacitated from making a contract, bills of exchange,

change, or promissory notes, shall not be good *as against them*, but such instruments will nevertheless be valid against all other parties competent to the instrument. Poth. Pl. 29; 2 Atk. 181, 182.

Although an infant cannot bind himself in a bill or note even for necessaries, his contract is not absolutely *void* but *voidable*, and it has been said that a promise to pay the bill made after he attained his majority, would be equally operative against him as if of full age at the time the contract was made. Sel. Ca. 166. 201; 1 T. R. 648. See *Infants, Married Women, Parties to negotiable instruments.*

BILLS OF EXCHANGE, *essentials to their validity.* These instruments must be *certain* in *payment,* and not depend on any particular event or contingency which may render such payment doubtful.—They must be for payment of *money only,* and not for the payment of money and performance of some other act, such contract not being negotiable as bills of exchange according to the custom of merchants. 3 Wells. 213; 4 Mod. 242; Bull. N, P. 272.

An instrument of the above description, although

although not negotiable, may nevertheless it is said support an action between the parties and be declared on between the original parties, as a bill. Per Kenyon, Ch. J. in Alves *v.* Hodson, 7 T. R. 243.

In cases however where *the time only of payment* is uncertain, the payment must be absolute, and *at some time or other.* Bills or notes upon such uncertainties with respect *to time* only have been held to be good: thus, in a contingent event of public notoriety respecting trade, &c. as if it be payable " two months after a certain ship is paid off," or on the receipt of the payee's wages due to him from a certain ship; or if a bill be drawn payable six weeks after the death of the drawer's father; or to an infant when he shall come of age, specifying the day when that event is to happen—such will be valid and negotiable bills.

Naming the fund also, " as an order ' to " pay a certain sum of money as my quarterly " halfpay by advance'—to pay a sum of money, &c. for value received out of the pre- " mises in Rosemary Lane," have been adjudged to be good bills. Ld. Raym. 1545; 7 T. R. 733.

A note also whereby the maker promised to

pay

pay "to A. B. 8*l.* so much being to be due from me to C. D. my landlady at Lady Day next, who is indebted in that sum to A. B." was judged not to be conditional, and consequently a good bill. Burn. 226.

B<small>ILLS OR</small> N<small>OTES</small> *given for goods, how far to be considered as good payment.* If the seller of goods agree to take bills as payment, and to run the risk of being paid, this will be considered as payment whether such bills have or have not been afterwards paid. 7 T. R. 66. See *Payment.*

B<small>ILLS OF</small> E<small>XCHANGE</small>, *or Promissory Notes, made abroad, requisites constituting their validity.* Bills or notes made in a foreign country must be conformable to the laws of the country where they are made in order to be of any validity in this country. Upon this ground, a promissory note without a stamp given to a sailor for payment of his wages on performance of a voyage, was judged to be void, the laws of Jamaica, where the instrument was made, requiring a stamp. Alves *v.* Hodson, 7 T. R. 231.

B<small>ILLS</small>, *or Notes, at what periods made payable.* Bills or notes may be made payable upon *demand,*

demand, or *at sight,* or at a certain period *after sight,* or at a certain period *after date.* If made payable a certain number of days after date, the day of the date is not included in the computation; therefore a bill dated on the 1st of May, at ten days after date, becomes due on the day of grace after the 11th. See *Computation of Time, Days of Grace, Style, Usance.*

B I L L S   O F   E X C H A N G E   *how far necessary to express " value received."* These words are by no means essential to the validity of a bill, but they are essential to obtain the benefit of the statute giving interest, damages, and costs. Evans, p. 11.

For further particulars upon this head, see *Acceptance, Date, Days of Grace, Indorsement, Stamp, &c. &c.*

C

CASH NOTES are notes originally given by bankers to their customers as an acknowledgment for money received to their use: these notes are seldom issued except by country bankers, the use of them being superseded in the Metropolis by the introduction of checks. If issued by bankers in London they are called *shop notes;* these are in form similar to common promissory notes payable to bearer on demand; and from being payable *to bearer or order on demand*, they are considered the same as cash; they are also, like bankers' checks, transferable by delivery only. They may notwithstanding be negotiable by indorsement, in which case they resemble a bill of exchange, and

G   may

may be declared upon accordingly as such against the indorser; in all other respects they are analogous to bills of exchange, and are governed by the same principle.

CHECKS OR DRAFTS ON BANKERS are instruments by means of which a creditor may assign to a *third person*, not originally party to a contract, the legal as well as equitable interest in a debt raised by it, so as to vest in such assignee a right of action against the original debtor. 1 H. B. 602. Being uniformly made payable *to bearer* constitutes a characteristic difference between these instruments and bills of exchange; and the legislature has considered them in a more favourable point of view by exempting them from the stamp duties. These instruments are equally negotiable with bills, although strictly speaking they are not due before payment is demanded. When given in payment they are considered as cash, and it is said may be declared upon as bills of exchange, and that when indorsed they are similar to bills of exchange; and the moment this resemblance begins, they are governed by the same principles of law as bills of exchange.

CHECKS *given by country bankers for payment*

of

of a sum of money in a bill at a given date. It is
observed by Mr. Evans, that the checks given
by merchants of Bristol and other commercial
places upon their bankers, directing them to
pay a certain sum of money in a bill at a given
date, have not any legal efficacy as negotiable
instruments; the essence of which is, that they
shall be for payment of money. Two cases,
however, have occurred, viz. Gregson *v.* Back-
house, and Bolton *v.* Richards, in the latter of
which it was held that such a check not being
presented in reasonable time, the debt was discharged. This case was as follows:—

A broker's clerk in Liverpool received a
check of this kind in payment for goods on
the 1st of ——————, drawn upon Caldwell and
Co. bankers in that place, and *gave a receipt
for the amount,* expressing it to be paid in a
bill at two months *from this day.* The check
was presented on the 2d, and a bill given *dated
on that day.* Bills at two months drawn by Caldwell and Co. on their correspondents Forbes
and Gregory *on the first* were paid; but on
the day corresponding with the *second* they
stopped payment. Different merchants were
examined respecting the usage of the place,
but

but their accounts were not exactly uniform. Mr. Justice Lawrence left the question to the Jury, whether the presentment was made in a reasonable time, and laid some stress upon the language of the receipt. The Jury found a verdict for the defendant.

CHECKS *payable on demand, or where no time of payment is expressed.* Such instruments are payable instantly on the presentment, without any indulgence or days of grace; but the presentment should be made within a *reasonable time* after the receipt, otherwise the holder not using due diligence to obtain payment, will be responsible, and the person from whom he received it will be discharged. Ld. Raym. 930.

CHECKS, *what shall be reasonable time for presentment.* It has been for some time matter of discussion what shall be deemed reasonable time for the presentment of a check or draft, and whether this shall be determined by the Court or Jury. According to the current of decisions it appears (Mr. Chitty observes in his treatise), that this should be left to a Jury to determine; but that the decisions of a Jury, although composed of mercantile men, were found so much at variance, that the Court, for the

the sake of certainty, has laid it down as a rule, that it is *for the Court*, and not for the Jury, to decide what shall be a reasonable time for presentment. 1 T. R. 168; Appleton *v.* Sweetapple, Bayl. 65. This doctrine is, however, by no means universally assented to. Doug. 515; 2 H. B. 568, 9.

In some cases, keeping a check *three, four,* or *five* days was held to be not too long. 2 Free. 247, 257. In another case it was held that presentment for payment must be made within *two* days, Str. 508; and in more recent decisions it has been adjudged that presentment should be made *the very day* the check is received. Chitty 147, cites 1 Bla. Rep. 168. Brown *v.* Collinson, Beawes' Pl. 229; Kyd 45; Appleton *v.* Sweetapple, Bayl. 65.

According to the opinion of merchants of the present day, a check on a banker ought to be presented for payment on *the same day* it is received, if given in the place where payable, and the distance or other circumstances will allow of it. But if this question is to be considered as dependent upon the usage of merchants as settled by judicial decisions, the result of these decisions is, that a presentment of a draft or a banker's check, payable in the place where it was given, may be made at any time before twelve o'clock on the *day after* the receipt of it, or at any time *within twenty-four hours* after such receipt. Str. 415, 416, 910, 1175, 1248; Ld. Raym. 928; Holt 120; 1 T. R. 168; Appleton *v.* Sweetapple, Bayl. 65; Brown *v.* Collinson, Beawes' Pl. 229; Kyd, 45.

From this species of uncertainty it appears in all cases adviseable for the holder of a check to present it, where circumstances will allow it, on the same day it is received. If the party reside at a distance, it is a general rule that it should be presented as soon as possible, and the time for presentment is governed by the same principles as those which regulate the notice for non-acceptance of a bill of exchange. See *Presentment.*

CHECK *given in payment of a bill.* If payment of a bill be made with a check, such payment will justify a person holding a bill in giving it up, although such check be afterwards dishonoured. 6 T. R. 12.

CHECK *if paid before due.* If paid before due, in case of loss or accident the banker must

must pay it over again. Da Silva *v.* Fuller, Sittings London, Easter 1776, Esp. Ni. Pri. 40. See *Loss, Robbery.*

CHECK *paid after notice of bankruptcy.* The check of a trader, if paid by a banker with whom he keeps cash after notice of the act of bankruptcy, will be void, and the assignees may bring an action to recover it either from the banker or payee of the check, if such payee had notice of the bankruptcy.

CLERK *of a Notary.* It appears doubtful whether the *clerk of a notary* be competent to note or protest an inland bill of exchange under 3 & 4 Ann. c. 9. § 5; 4 T. R. 174; Ld. Raym. 743.

COMMISSION.—This is an allowance for discount, which in the French law is termed provision. It is usual for country banks to charge five shillings or ten shillings per cent. commission upon the bills which they discount, or any money which passes through their hands. This was once supposed to be usurious, but is now decided to be a lawful charge, being a reasonable compensation for their trouble, and for the capital which they employ in providing cash to answer such exigencies.

COMMISSION OF BANKRUPT. Any person having a right of action upon any bill of exchange or analogous instrument, has a right to prove his debt under a commission of bankrupt.

Creditors by bill, note, or other security payable at a future day, may, by 5 G. II. c. 30, take out a commission *before* the day of payment. A person to whom a bill or note is indorsed after an act of bankruptcy committed, is authorised to take out a commission, the debt subsisting before the act of bankruptcy, though in the person of a different creditor, Glaister *v.* Hewer, 7 T. R. 498. See *Bankrupt, Bankruptcy, Dividend, Proof.*

COMPANY, *incorporated.* See *Corporation, Partners.*

COMPARISON OF HANDS is not admissible evidence in a court to prove the signature of any of the parties to a bill of exchange or promissory note. See *Evidence.*

COMPOSITION WITH THE ACCEPTOR.—If the holder of a bill of exchange *compound* with the acceptor, without the assent of the other parties, he by such conduct releases all the other parties from their responsibility. Cooke's Bank. Laws 168.

'COMPOSITION *by payee, how far excluding him from notice.* If the payee lend his name to secure a composition from the drawer to a creditor, and take effects of the drawer to answer it, he is not entitled to notice. **De Bert** *v.* Atkinson.

COMPUTATION OF TIME.—If a bill be drawn at a place using one style, and payable at a day certain at a place using another, the time it is said must be computed according to the usage of the country where the bill is drawn, because the contract raised by the making of a bill of exchange is understood to have been made at that place, and should consequently be calculated according to the laws of it, Bayl. 68, otherwise according to the style of the place where it is payable. In the former case, the date must be reduced or carried forward to the style of the place where the bill is payable, and the time reckoned from thence, Mar. p. 22. Thus on a bill dated the 1st of March old style, and payable here one month after date, the time must be computed from the 19th of February new style; and on a bill dated the 19th of February new style, and payable at Petersburgh one month after date, from the 1st of March old style.

COMPUTATION *by months*. When the time after the expiration of which a bill is payable is limited by months, the calculation is always made by *calendar* and not *lunar* months; thus on a bill or note payable one month after date, and dated the *first* day of January, the month will not expire until the *first* of February.

COMPUTATION *by days*. When the time is computed by days, the day on which the event happens is to be excluded. Bellasis *v.* Hester, Ld. Raym. 280; Lutw. 1591.

Thus on a bill or note payable ten days after date, dated the 1st of January, the time does not expire, with the addition of the three days of grace, until the 14th.

COMPUTATION *when bill not dated*. Where a bill or check is drawn payable at usance, or a certain time after date, and it is not dated, the time when it is payable must be computed from the day it issued, exclusive thereof, Bayl. 68, cites Ld. Raym. 1076. See *Days of grace, Usance*.

CONDITIONAL ACCEPTANCE. See *Acceptance conditional*.

CONSIDERATION.—All bills of ex-change carry with them the same internal evidence

dence of a consideration as contracts evidenced by bonds and other specialties. Upon this ground it is scarcely ever necessary for the plaintiff in an action upon a bill of exchange to prove that he gave a consideration for it; and it is in no instance open to the defendant to prove that he received no consideration, unless in an action brought against him by the person with whom he was *immediately* concerned in the negotiation of the instrument. 1 Bla. Rep. 445.

CONSIDERATION *legal.* A debt of a third person, or a debt barred by the statute of limitations, by a discharge under an insolvent or fugitive act, by a bankruptcy and certificate, or by a composition, are good considerations, Popplewell *v.* Wilson, Str. 294; Ld. Raym. 389; 6 Mod. 309; Burr. 2630; Blackst. 703; Cowp. 290; Trueman *v.* Fenton, Cowp. 544; Birch *v.* Sharland, 1 T. R. 715; Cowp. 290. Past seduction has been deemed a good consideration, Turner *v.* Vaughan, 2 Wils. 339.

CONSIDERATIONS *illegal.* Dropping a criminal prosecution, or suppressing evidence thereon, a recommendation to an office in the king's household (though of a private nature, and not within the statute of the 5th & 6th

Edw.

Edw. III.), a *smuggling*, *usurious*, *or stock-jobbing* contract, have been deemed illegal considerations, 3 P. Wms. 279; Harrington *v.* Du Chatel, Bro. C. C. 114; Guichard *v.* Roberts, Blackst. 445; 12 Anne, st. 2. c. 16; 7 Geo. II. c. 8.

By 9 Anne, c. 14, § 1, money lost by gaming, or betting on the sides of persons so gaming, money knowingly lent for such gaming or betting, or money lent at the time and place of such play, to any person either then gaming or betting, or who shall during the play play or bet, is an illegal consideration.

Cricket, horse-racing, or foot-racing against time, are considered as games; insuring in the lottery, not. Jeffryes *v.* Watts, 1 Wils. 220; Lynall *v.* Longbotham, 2 Wils. 36; Lewis *v.* Piercy, 1 H. Bl. 29.

CONSIDERATION, *when the want of it cannot be insisted upon.* Any person having received a consideration cannot insist upon the want of one if the plaintiff as any intermediate party between him and the defendant took the bill or note *bona fide*, and upon a good consideration. Morris *v.* Lee, B. R. H. 26 G. 3.

CONSIDERATION *upon an accommodation bill.*

In

In case of an accommodation bill, such circumstance is known to the indorsee, and he
pays only *part* of the amount, he can in this
case only recover the sum he has actually paid
for the bill, Esp. Ni. Pri. 261; but where a
bill is given for money really due from the
drawee to the drawer, or is drawn in the regular course of business, the indorsee in such
case, although he has not given the indorser
the full amount of the bill, may nevertheless
recover the whole, and be the holder of the
overplus above the sum he has actually paid to
the use of the indorser. Esp. Ca. Ni. Pri. 261.

CONSIDERATIONS *valuable, when party
giving it cannot recover.* Where a third person
gives a valuable consideration for a bill, knowing it to be founded upon any of the abovemen-
tioned illegal considerations, he cannot recover upon it. Esp. Ca. Ni. Pri. 166.

CONSIDERATION *the illegality of, when it
may be insisted upon.* In those cases where the
legislature has declared that the illegality of the
consideration shall make the bill or note absolutely void, as in the case of signing a bankrupt's certificate, gaming, or usury, the defendant may insist upon such illegality though

H the

the plaintiff, or some party between him and the defendant, took the bill *bona fide*, and gave a valuable consideration for it, Str. 1155. But unless where it has been expressly declared by the legislature that the illegality of the consideration shall render the instrument void, the illegality of the consideration cannot be set up as a defence in an action brought by a *bona fide* holder, Sel. Ca. 71; and if the consideration upon which the bill was given originally was not so illegal as to render the instrument absolutely void, a subsequent illegal consideration of any description, given as the transfer, will not invalidate the instrument in the hands of a *bona fide* holder. Esp. Ca. Ni. Pri. 274.

CONSIDERATION *illegal, when not to be set aside.* If the defendant suffer a judgment to go by default, upon a bill founded upon an illegal consideration, he will be precluded from the opportunity of objecting to the sufficiency of the consideration. Shepherd *v.* Charter, 4 T. R. 275.

CONSTRUCTION *of negotiable instruments.* Courts of law, in consequence of the commercial importance of bills, have always most liberally construed them to be made effective according

according to the intention of the parties, which
should be rendered operative according to the
law of the country where the contract is made,
and not according to the law of that country
into which any or all the parties may remove.
The computation of time for payment is, however, in general, to be calculated according to
the laws of that country where the bill is made
payable, Beawes' Pl. 251; Mar. 102. A bill
of exchange is considered as having been made
at the place where it is payable, and consequently the contract should be construed and
regulated according to the laws and usages of
that place to which the contracting parties have
understood themselves subject. Poth. Pl. 155.
sed qu.?

CONSTRUCTION *of bills, how different from
that of deeds*. In construing bills of exchange
the Courts have followed a different rule than
in the construction of deeds; in the latter the
words and language must bear the sense which
is attemped to be put upon them, and therefore in an action brought by the indorsee against
the acceptor, and he could not prove an indorsement by the payee, evidence was admitted
to prove that the payee was a *fictitious* person,
and consequently could not indorse the instrument;

ment; it was therefore adjudged that as the drawer and acceptor knew of this fact, the bill should operate against them as a bill originally payable to bearer, and the holder might recover against them as such. 1 K. B. 569.

CONTINGENCY.—On account of the perplexity which would be thereby introduced into commercial transactions, bills or notes must not be made payable upon a contingency, they must, on the contrary, be made for the payment of a sum of *money certainly*, and *at all events*, otherwise they are not to be considered as negotiable instruments within the custom of merchants. It has however been held, that such instruments, although not *negotiable as bills*, may nevertheless be declared upon as such between the original parties to it, per Kenyon, Ch. J. in Alves *v.* Hodgson, 7 T. R. 243. See *Bills of Exchange*.

CONTRACT.—The contract in negotiable instruments is supposed to be made in the country where the instrument is made, the form of the remedy must nevertheless depend upon the laws of that country where such remedy is procured. See *Obligation, Liability, Remedy.*

COR-

CORPORATIONS may become parties to bills of exchange through the medium of their agents; with respect however to drawing bills, by 6th Anne, c. 22, § 9, and 15 G. 2. c. 13, § 13, it is enacted, that no corporation or partnership exceeding *six* persons in number (except the Governor and Company of the Bank of England), shall borrow, owe, or take up any sum or sums of money payable on demand at any less time than six months from the borrowing thereof.

COSTS.—With respect to bills of exchange or promissory notes, in case of dishonour, the acceptor of the one or maker of the other are responsible to the holder for all costs incurred by any of the subsequent parties. In an action against the indorser, drawer, or acceptor of a bill, if he has any defence he pleads, if none, he either compromises the action or suffers judgment to go by default. If it be a *bona fide* bill, the least expensive and least troublesome mode is, to obtain a Judge's order grounded upon summons to stay proceedings upon payment of debt and costs. If separate actions are brought against the acceptor, drawer, and indorser, at the same time, the Court will stay proceedings, in any stage of the action, against

H 2   the

the drawer or any one of the indorsers, upon payment of the amount of the bill and the costs of that particular action; but the action against the acceptor will only be stayed on the terms of his paying the costs in all the actions he being the original defaulter. 1 T. R. 691; Str. 515; Bla. Rep. 749.

CREDIT.—Any holder of a bill of exchange undertaking to give longer credit than such bill warrants upon the face of it, stands responsible for all consequences, and, by making the bill his own, releases all parties but the acceptor from their responsibility. If, therefore, the holder of a bill neglect to present it to the drawee at the time it becomes due, or, where no time is expressed, within a reasonable time after the receipt of the instrument, he shall not afterwards be permitted to resort to the drawer or indorser, whose respective contracts are collateral only to pay in default of the drawee, and not immediate and absolute like that of the acceptor, and who are always presumed to have sustained damage in consequence of the laches or neglect of the holder. 1 Salk. 127; Str. 1087; Bull. Ni. Pri. 470; 2 Black. Com. 470; Poth. Pl. 129; 7 T. R. 581, 582. See *Holder*, *Notice*, *Presentment*.

D.

DAMAGE.—The holder of a bill of exchange, in excuse for any omission to give notice of the non-acceptance or non-payment of a bill of exchange, must prove that the person insisting upon the want of it did not sustain any damage, or must adduce such evidence as may afford an inference to that effect, and thereby throw the *onus probandi* upon such person complaining of the want of notice.

DAMAGE. If an acceptance be made payable at a banker's, and it has not been presented there by the holder, if the acceptor can prove that he has sustained any damage from such neglect, the acceptor will be discharged from his liability, Str. 1198; *sed qu.?* See *Presentment for Payment*.

DAMAGE

DAMAGE *in bills returned protested from India.* A person discounted a bill in India for 2800 pagodas at six guineas a pagoda, and it appeared that it was the constant course of trade, with respect to bills returned protested from India, to allow at the rate of 10*s.* the pagoda, and 5*l.* per cent. upon the amount, after thirty days' notice of non-payment, which includes interest, exchange, and all other charges. This was objected to as usurious, but was allowed as fair and reasonable by the Court of Kings Bench. Auriol *v.* Thomas, 2 T. R. 52; Evans 61, 62.

DAMAGE *recoverable in America upon bills drawn in this country.* By a law of Pennsylvania it was provided, that if any person should draw or indorse any bill on Europe which should be returned protested for non-payment, the drawer and all others concerned should pay the contents, together with 20*l.* per cent. for damage. And it was decided by Lord Hardwicke, that a person here who had authorised his creditor in Pennsylvania to draw upon him was liable to the drawer for the money which he had paid in pursuance of this law, the same as if it had been by an express stipulation, and that it

was

was a debt proveable under his commission. Ambler, 672. From this it may be observed generally, that the laws of other countries relative to negotiable instruments within their jurisdiction, are supported by the English Courts upon a principle of the law of nations.

DAMAGES, *nature of those recoverable upon dishonour of negotiable instruments.* The amount of damages to be recovered by the plaintiff in consequence of the dishonour of a bill of exchange are the sum for which the bill is payable, *interest* in certain cases, and such expences as may have been occasioned by the dishonour, such as re-exchange, postage, &c. With respect to the principal money, no more can be recovered than is actually due upon the face of the instrument.* See *Instalments, Interest, Expences, Postage, Re-exchange, Provision, Charges.*

DAMAGES *upon bills payable by instalments.* See *Instalments.*

DATE.—It becomes necessary, as the time of payment is to be regulated by the date of the instrument, that this should be clearly expressed, and although it has been the common practice to use figures for this purpose, yet as these

* [By the laws of several of the United States, the following damages are recoverable on Foreign bills returned. The New-England States, 10 per cent. New-Jersey, no damages specified; Pennsylvania, 20 per cent. Maryland, 15 per cent.]

these will admit of alteration either through accident or design much more easily than words, which would invalidate the instrument in the hands of an innocent holder, it would be more adviseable to write the date in words at full length, Beawes' Pl. 3. and Mar. 2d Ed. 914; 4 T. R. 320. A date, however, except in the case of bills or drafts for the payment of twenty shillings or above, and less than five pounds, 17 Geo. 3. c. 30. (see *Small Note Bill)*, is not an essentially component part of a bill of exchange; for where a bill has no date if the time be necessary to be enquired into, it shall be computed from the day it was issued, 2 Ld. Raym. 1076; 4 T. R. 337; Bac. Abr. tit. Leases, L. 1; Com. Dig. tit. Fact, B. 3.

DATE *the day of, in what cases to be reckoned exclusively.* In bills payable at usance so many days after sight, or *from* the date, the day of acceptance or of the date must be excluded, Ld. Raym. 280; 6 T. R. 212; Beawes' Pl. 252. *acc.* Mayo *v.* Cooper, Fort. 376. *contra.*

DATE *of a protest,* should be on the last day of grace, being the day when the bill becomes due, 4 T. R. 170. See *Protest.*

DAY *upon which acceptance is made, when*
necessary

necessary to be written. This is necessary upon all bills payable *after sight.*

DAYS OF GRACE are certain days after the time limited by the bill, which the acceptor has a right to demand for payment of the bill; these days were so called because they were formerly gratuitously allowed, but now by the custom of merchants, sanctioned by the decisions of Courts of Justice, they are demandable of right. The number of these days varies according to the custom of different countries. Within the United Kingdom *three* days grace are allowed, in other countries more. If the last of the *three* days happen upon a Sunday, the bill becomes payable on the Saturday. [Same custom in all the U. S.]

DAYS OF GRACE, *how to be computed.* These days must always be computed according to the laws and customs of the place where the bill becomes due. Thus at Hamburgh the day when the bill becomes due makes one of the days of grace; but this mode of computation is peculiar to Hamburgh. In Great Britain, Ireland, France, Amsterdam, Rotterdam, Antwerp, Middleburgh, Dantzick, and Koningsburg, Sundays and Holidays are always included

cluded in the days of grace, but they are not at Venice, Cologne, Breslau, and Nuremburg. In this country, if the third day of grace happen on a Sunday or great holiday, as Christmas-day, upon which no bills used to be paid, the party should demand the money upon the second day of grace; and in case it is not then paid, the holder is immediately to consider the bill as dishonoured, Chitty on Bills, p. 140, cites Ld. Raym. 374: Mar. 96; in other cases, a presentment before the third day of grace is considered as a mere nullity, Esp. Ca. Ni. Pri. 261.

It does not appear to be determined whether days of grace are allowed upon bills payable at sight. It is observed by Pothier, that a bill payable at sight is payable as soon as the bearer presents it to the drawee, and Beawes, in his Lex Mercatoria observes, that bills made payable here at sight have no days of grace allowed, but that it would be otherwise in case of bills payable *one* day after sight. It is observed by Mr. Montefiore, a judicious Conveyancer and Notary Public, in the Appendix to his volume of Commercial and Notarial Precedents, that a bill payable at sight is in fact synonymous

synonymous with a bill payable on demand, and as such it is considered and acted upon by the merchants and bankers of this country.

The practice of merchants and bankers is certainly entitled to respect, but a principle established by judicial decisions is entitled at least to equal consideration. All the writers upon this branch of jurisprudence (Mr. Montefiore excepted) are coincident in expressing a doubt upon this point; and the weight of judicial decision and high authority, if they do not make the scale preponderate in favour of the affirmative of this question, are at least sufficient to raise a doubt upon the subject.

In the case of Dehers *v.* Harriet, Shower 163, cited by Mr. Chitty, it was taken for granted that days of grace are allowable upon a bill payable on demand, and the same point was also decided in the case of Coleman *v.* Sayer, 1 Barnard's Reports B. R. 303; Vin. Ab. tit. Bills of Exchange, B. J. Anson *v.* Thomas, B. R. T. 24 G. 3. Bayl. 23, *n. b.* and in another case, where in an action upon an inland bill payable at sight the question was, whether it was included under an exception in the stamp act of 23 G. 3. c. 49. § 4. in favour of bills payable on demand, the Court held it

I was

was not, and Mr. Justice Buller upon that occasion mentioned a case before Chief Justice Willes, which was tried in London, in which a Jury of Merchants was of opinion that the usual days of grace were to be allowed upon bills payable at sight, J. Anson *v.* Thomas, B. R. T. 24 G. 3. cited by Bailey and Chitty.

DAYS OF GRACE, *how far the acceptor is allowed the last moment of the last day of grace.* This point was incidentally discussed in the case of Leftly *v.* Mills, 4 T. R. 170. See *Payment.*

DAYS OF PUBLIC REST *not to be reckoned in computing the time of payment of negotiable instruments.* If the last day of grace should fall on Sunday, or a day of public rest, the instrument will become due on the day preceding. The only days of rest which are publicly recognised in this country, except Sunday, are Christmas-day and Good Friday, the latter expressly by 40 Geo. 3. and probably although the point has never been litigated, days appointed by his Majesty's proclamation for public fasts or thanksgivings would be thus specially privileged. A late writer submits upon this subject the following query:—Supposing
. the

the *third day* should fall on Sunday the 26th of
December, whether, on account of Christmas-
day falling on the *Saturday*, only *one* day of
grace would be allowed, and the bill become
payable on the Friday, or whether *four* days
would be allowed, and the time be extended to
Monday?

DEATH *of the Holder* of a bill of exchange
or his agent will be an excuse for the want of a
regular notice of the non-acceptance or non-
payment of a bill of exchange, provided such
notice is given *as soon as possible after the impediment is removed;* and it is said that his executor, although he has not proved the will, must
present the bill to the drawee, for the right of
transfer in such case devolves to the executor
or administrator of the holder; in which case,
however, such personal representative would
become personally liable in case of a deficiency
of the testator or intestate's estate, because
such transfer is in law considered as an admission of assets. 3 Wils. 1; Str. 1260; 2 Barnes
137. cites Bur. 1225; 1 T. R. 487; 1 H. B.
622.

Although the drawer or indorsers, it is said,
would be chargeable in case of the sudden
death

death of the holder of the bill, in consequence of want of presentment (especially if payment would have been made upon a presentment in proper time), Mr. Evans nevertheless expresses some doubt, at least, upon the equity of this principle; for he observes, that although it be admitted that there is no laches in the holder, it must, he says, be equally observed that there is no laches in the other parties, and their engagement is only that a bill shall be paid if regularly presented. The accidents which occur, though unaccompanied by any fault, should fall upon the owner of the property affected by them, and not upon others who are equally innocent.

DEATH *of the drawee*. Although it has been said that this will be a good excuse to the holder, the thing stipulated for having, by the act of God, become impossible; and although upon the authority of Molloy and Pothier Mr. Chitty observes that the holder should in this case enquire his personal representative, and there present the instrument; yet it is judiciously observed by Mr. Evans, that under these circumstances the true course seems to be to give immediate notice, in order that the drawer

may

may remit a proper sum for payment. Mr. Evans further observes, that he does not think the representatives can be properly required to accept, for they are not bound to enter into a personal obligation, and cannot by any acceptance affect the property of the deceased, Evans, p. 51. It has been decided that provided the drawee *has assets*, his death will be no excuse for the want of notice, Russel *v.* Langstaffe, Doug. 497, 515; 1 T. R. 498; 2 T. R. 336; 2 H. B. 612. In all cases, whether of death, bankruptcy, loss, or other accident, it is adviseable and regular to give notice, which can only be dispensed with under circumstances peculiarly special, where the notice has been rendered impossible, or where none of the parties to the instrument can reasonably complain of the want of it.

DEBT *upon a negotiable instrument, when supposed to be contracted.* In the case of Macarty *v.* Barrow, Str. 994; 3 Wils. 17, it was laid down by Lord Mansfield that the drawer of a bill contracted a debt at the very moment he drew it, and that the non-acceptance or protest did not raise any debt, but was only notice to the holder that the drawee could not pay the

same,

same, consequently that the debt was proveable upon an intervening bankruptcy, and barred by the certificate.

DEBT, see *Action of Debt.*

DEBT *action of, its advantages.* See *Action of Debt.*

DECLARATION *upon a note or bill of exchange.* The declaration may be founded either upon the instrument itself, with the addition of the common counts (which is most usual), or upon the consideration of the instrument, in which latter case the plaintiff declares upon the common money counts, or such of them as are adapted to the circumstances of the case, and may give the instrument in evidence to support his action.

DECLARATION, *what it must state.* A declaration must state the contract and how it arose—the breach of such contract—the title of the plaintiff to recover—and it concludes by praying relief for the damages sustained by such breach.

DECLARATION, *how it should set forth the instrument.* The instrument should be stated in the declaration as it was really made; any variance in this respect (except under special circum-

circumstances, where the rules of law prevent the instrument declared on to operate according to the words of it, such as where bills payable to fictitious persons may be stated as payable to bearer, against every person aware of that fail, Bristow *v.* Wright, Doug. 667.) will be fatal. In stating the instrument it is not usual to state more of it than is necessary to entitle the plaintiff to recover.

DECLARATION, *how it should set forth the contract.* The plaintiff in his declaration must set forth the contract, and how the defendant made himself a party to it, whether by *making*, *accepting*, *indorsing*, or *delivering* the instrument *personally* or by *his agent;* in which latter case it is usual to state that either of these acts was done by the procuration of the agent properly authorised and employed for the purpose, 1 H. B. 313; 6 T. R. 659.

DECLARATION, *how it should set forth the plaintiff's title.* The plaintiff suing upon any instrument must shew a sufficient title to enable him to maintain the action, 4 T. R. 471. Thus in an action by the assignee of a bill, it is incumbent upon the plaintiff to shew that the instrument authorises a transfer, except under special

special circumstances similar to the above stated with respect to the instrument; thus the payee of an instrument to his *own order* may state it to have been made payable to himself, 2 Show. 8. In stating the title of the plaintiff it is customary to state it as warranted by the instrument itself; and if he be a remote indorsee, to set forth the several indorsements; in cases, however, where the first indorsement is *in blank*, and the plaintiff is doubtful whether he can prove all the intermediate indorsements, it is usual to add a count stating the plaintiff as the immediate indorsee of the first indorser, and to strike out all the intermediate indorsers at the time of trial, Peacock *v.* Rhodes, Doug. 633 ; Holl. 296 ; Kyd, 206. An indorsee may declare against his immediate indorser, as on a bill of exchange *made* by the defendant, directed to the acceptor, and payable to the plaintiff, the act of indorsing being similar to making a new bill.

DECLARATION, *in case of a conditional acceptance*, must state the event to have taken place. It is not necessary to allege that the instrument was delivered, it will be sufficient to allege that it was made. 7 T. R. 596.

DECLARA-

DECLARATION. *Utility of adding the common counts.* These should be added because they will in many cases supply the place of the count upon the instrument itself, and by adding these the plaintiff will be at liberty to go into the consideration upon which the instrument was given, and may recover upon the common counts, if the special count on the instrument should be found defective, or the proof should fail in the facts necessary to support it; thus where the plaintiff declared on a promissory note, and a *quantum meruit* for work and labour, which was the consideration of the note, but the instrument not being duly stamped could not be read in evidence, and a verdict having been taken generally for the plaintiff, the Court thought the plaintiff ought to have an opportunity of recovering upon the other count, and granted a new trial, 7 T. R. 241; and in Wilson *v.* Kennedy, where the same point was determined, Lord Kenyon said that a promissory note was not like a bond, which merged the demand. Esp. 245.

DECLARATION, *when the count for money lent should be added.* In an action at the suit of the payee of a bill of exchange against the
drawer,

drawer, and an action at the suit of the payee of a promissory note against the maker, the count for money lent should be added, as being evidence of money lent by the payee to the drawer of the one and the maker of the other. Str. 725; Bayl. 95; 6 T. R. 123. This count is also proper to be subjoined to the special one in an action at the suit of the indorsee against his immediate indorser. Kessebower *v.* Tims, B. R. E. 22 G. 3. Bayl. 96. *n. b.*

DECLARATION UPON BILLS, *how differing from that upon promissory notes.* In declaring upon a promissory note it is usual to state that the defendant became liable by force of the statute of Anne, which renders these instruments negotiable. 4 T. R. 155. The above statute, however, has been held to be only a *concurrent* remedy; it is consequently not necessary for the plaintiff, although it is usual, to declare on the note; but in an action for money lent the same may be given in evidence. In declaring either upon bills or notes, reference to the custom in any part of the declaration has been, though usual, deemed unnecessary. Ld. Raym. 1542. Nor is it necessary to state an express promise, such being always implied wherever

wherever there is a legal liability. Carth. 509;
Salk. 128; Hard. 53, 486.

DEFENCE *to an action upon a bill or note.*
The defence to an action upon a negotiable
instrument may be founded upon the following facts, viz.—A mis-statement in the
declaration—denial of the contract, or that the
defendant was a party to it in the manner
stated—the invalidity of the contract on account of the illegality of the considerations
upon which it was founded—or from incapacity of the parties to bind themselves—discharge of the contract, or an excuse for non-
performance of it—and disability of the plaintiff to sue, or protection of the defendant from
being sued.

DEFENCE, *arising from mis-statement in the
declaration.* Those defences arising from in-
formality, such as a mis-statement in the declaration of the original cause of action, may
be taken advantage of by a general or special
demurrer. The latter, and by far the more
numerous species, may be either advanced in
the shape of a special plea, or given in evidence
under the general issue.

DEFENCE *arising from a denial of the contract.*
This species of defence denies that the instrument

ment declared upon was *made*, *indorsed*, or *ac-cepted;* or that the defendant was a party to it. This defence, which amounts to the general issue, may be taken advantage of by the plea of *non assumpsit*, which puts the plaintiff upon the proof of the facts as stated in his declaration.

DEFENCES *admitting the contract, but alleging that the contract was void or voidable.* Those defences which admit the contract, but allege it to be void, are founded either upon the want of consideration—the illegality of the consideration—or the incapacity of the parties to bind themselves by such contract. Defences founded upon *illegal considerations* are those which allege *gaming*, *smuggling*, *stock-jobbing*, *usurious* or *vicious engagements* (such as future prostitution, &c.), some of which are absolutely void, and others voidable.

DEFENCES *arising from voidable contracts.* These are infancy or coverture, which may be given in evidence under the general issue or pleaded specially. With respect, however, to those cases where the circumstances of the defence lay more in the knowledge of the defendant than of the plaintiff, as in the case of infancy or coverture, it is not only fairer but

more

more advantageous, either to plead these, or to give notice of them to the plaintiff previous to the trial, otherwise a new trial will frequently be granted, the expences of which may ultimately fall upon the defendant.

DEFENCES *which admit the contract but allege an excuse for non-performance.* These allege negligence in the holder, such as want of presentment, or any other act whereby he is precluded from bringing his action.

DEFENCES *which allege a discharge of the contract, or an excuse for non-performance.* These are negligence, accord and satisfaction, arbitrament, release, former recovery, tender, set off, or the statute of limitation, notice, presentment, &c. whereby the plaintiff has precluded himself from his right of action.

DEFENCES *which allege the disability of the plaintiff to sue, or exemption of the defendant from being sued.* The former of these is where the plaintiff is an outlaw, alien, enemy, or bankrupt, or that the defendant is a bankrupt, or insolvent.

DEFENCES *which need not be pleaded.* Such defences which amount to a denial that the plaintiff had cause of action, are not pleaded,

K but

but given in evidence under the general issue, which puts the plaintiff upon proving his case.

DEFENCES *which must in all cases be pleaded.* It is customary to plead in all cases where the defendant admits that the plaintiff once had a right of action; but it is in all cases indispensable to plead *bankruptcy, insolvency, tender, set off,* or the *statute of limitations.*

DEFENCE, *what will not constitute one for the acceptor.* The want of presentment of a bill at the precise time when due, nor even before the commencement of an action, nor an indulgence to any of the other parties, will be no defence in an action against the acceptor. Esp. Ni. Pr. 46; Bayl. 78, *n. b.* 108, *n. a.*

DELAY, *how far admissible.* It is incumbent upon the holder of a negotiable instrument to use all diligence in procuring payment, or to give notice of refusal of acceptance or payment to the parties interested. Such delays, however, as are warranted by the common course of business, or occasioned by keeping a bill in circulation at a distance from the place where it is payable, have been held to be not improper; but any delay by keeping a bill locked up for any length of time, is not warrantable.

rantable. 2 H. Bl. 569; Muilman *v.* D'Égui-
no, 2 H. Bl. 565.

DELIVERY. A bill or note payable to A.
or *bearer* requires no indorsement, but is assignable by delivery only; and instruments originally payable to *order*, and indorsed so as to be
payable to bearer, may be assigned either by
indorsement and delivery, or delivery without
any indorsement. On a transfer by delivery
only, the person making it ceases to be a party
to the instrument. Ld. Raym. 442, 724, 929,
930; 3 Salk. 68; Combe 57: As long as the
first indorsement remains in blank, the instrument, as against the payee, the drawer, or acceptor, is assignable by mere delivery only,
notwithstanding it may have upon it subsequent
full indorsements. Smith *v.* Clarke, Peake 225.

DELIVERY *in case of loss or robbery.* A
transfer by delivery will convey a title to a bill
or note, if assignable by mere delivery, in case of
loss or theft, and the finder or stealer may convey a good title to such instrument. See *Loss,
Robbery.*

DELIVERY, *the obligation implied by it.* A
transfer by delivery, if made for an antecedent
debt, implies an undertaking from the indorser
to

to the person to whom it is transferred, and every other subsequent transferree, exactly similar to that which is implied by drawing a bill, except that in case of a note the stipulations with respect to the responsibility of the drawer, do not apply.

DEMAND *of acceptance of foreign and inland bills, how to be made.* See *Presentment for Acceptance, Protest, Payment, Acceptance.*

DEMAND *of payment.* This need not be personal; it will be sufficient if made at the place by him appointed for payment, or of his agent who has been accustomed to pay money for him. Esp. 512. [2 H. Bl. Rep. 509.]

DEMAND *of payment in case of death or removal.* See *Death of the Acceptor, Presentment, Removal.*

DISCHARGE. See *Release, Dishonour, Notice, Protest, Receipt, Satisfaction.*

DISCHARGE, *how far delay in presenting an acceptance payable at a banker's will operate as such.* Where an acceptance was made payable at a certain banker's, and the bill was kept an unreasonable time after it became due, and the banker failed, it was held that the acceptor was discharged. The principle of this decision was probably

probably that such an acceptance was considered, to a certain extent, as equivalent to a
check upon the banker, and the delay in presenting it induced the same consequences as a
delay in presenting a common check. In a
subsequent case, however, it was decided not
to be necessary in an action against the acceptor to prove a presentment at a banker's, no
special damage having arisen from any failure.
Bayl. 78; Esp. 115; Chit. 134. See *Discharge,*
Payment, Satisfaction.

DISCHARGE *by bail of the maker of a note.* If
a promissory note be discharged by the bail of
the maker, this will be a discharge of all the
other parties; and under such circumstances
it has been decided that the indorsee cannot
afterwards sue the indorser for the use of such
bail. 1 Wils. 46.

DISCHARGE *in case of payment for honour.*
Any person may make a payment of a negotiable instrument for the honour of the drawer or
indorsers, and such payment will be a discharge to all deriving a title under the person
for whose honour it is made, but will give the
party paying a right of indemnity against that
person and all who are answerable over to him.

DISCHARGE *from the holder of a bill, its operation with respect to the obligation.* The holder of a bill being entitled to the respective credits of all the other parties for the same sum, may, as a necessary consequence of this right, give a discharge to any of them; but a discharge to the acceptor, either before or after the bill becomes due, is a complete extinction of all the credit under the bill, and it has no longer any legal operation, at least so far as respects the rights of the person giving such discharge.

DISCHARGE *to the last indorser, its operation.* A discharge to the last indorser will not operate in favour of the preceding, nor of the drawer, nor acceptor, nor will in general the release to the drawer discharge the acceptor— nor if the holder take a prior indorser in execution, and afterwards liberate him out of custody, this will be no discharge to the subsequent indorser. 2 Bl. Rep. 1235.

DISCHARGE, *what will amount to this, by whom to be decided.* This is a question merely of fact, and consequently what will amount to an assent of the holder to discharge the acceptor, and of course all the other parties, is a question for the decision of the Jury, arising

out

out of the circumstances of the particular case. See *Satisfaction*, *Waiver*. For cases of construction upon this point, see Doug. 247.

DISCHARGE, *how far bills or notes given in payment shall be considered as a discharge of an antecedent debt*. Bills or notes are to be considered as *good payment of an antecedent debt*, provided they be duly honoured. Kearslake *v.* Morgan, 5 T. R. 513, and Richardson *v.* Rickman, cited *ibid*. If, however, *these are not paid*, they are to be considered as mere nullity. Upon this principle it was adjudged, that where a defendant was arrested, and discharged out of custody upon giving a draft which was refused acceptance, that the proceedings were perfectly regular in re-taking him upon the same writ. 6 T. R. 54. No action, however, can be maintained upon the original demand until these instruments have become payable. See *Payment*, *Satisfaction*.

DISCHARGE, *how far to be considered as good with respect to bills or checks given in payment*. By the statute of 3 & 4 Anne, any person accepting such bills as had been referred to in a preceding section in satisfaction of a former debt, it shall be accounted a full payment, if the

the person accepting them does not take his due course to obtain payment thereof by endeavouring to get the same accepted and paid, and make his protest either for non-acceptance or non-payment.

The above applies only to inland bills; but the principle of law is the same in all negotiable securities: thus, where a person received a note in payment, payable a few days after date, which he held four months, and in the interim the person upon whom the order was payable became insolvent, 2 Wils. 353; and in a more recent case, at Lancaster Assizes 1795, where a check given in payment, through negligence in its presentment, was held to be a sufficient discharge. See *Extinguishment, Notice, Satisfaction, Waiver;* see also 6 T. R. 139.

DISCOUNT. No action can be brought upon transfer by delivery only, merely by way of sale of the bill, as in the course of a discount. 3 T. R. 757; Esp. Ca. N. P. 447. See *Commission.*

DISSOLUTION OF PARTNERSHIP. See *Partnership.*

DIVIDEND. Taking a dividend under a commission against the acceptor will not discharge

charge the several parties to the instrument from their respective obligations to the holder, provided he has been guilty of no laches, and given regular notice of non-payment to the parties entitled to such notice. See *Bankruptcy*, *Proof.*

DIVIDEND, *what may be received by the holder under a commission against the other parties.* Where different parties to negotiable instruments have become bankrupts, Mr. Evans conceives that the holder is entitled to prove for the *full* amount of the respective debts, and receive dividends for the full amount upon the respective proofs, *although exceeding twenty shillings* in the pound: as, for example, if the holder prove upon the estate of the indorser, and receive *fifteen shillings in the pound* and a dividend is afterwards made on the part of the acceptor, of the like amount, he is to receive the *fifteen shillings* and pay *ten* shillings to the assignees of the indorser, who is only to be ultimately charged with the deficiency of the acceptor. If the dividend of fifteen shillings in the pound is first paid by the acceptor, and afterwards by the indorser, he can only receive the deficiency. It sometimes happens, from want of knowledge or attention, that the full

dividends

dividends are paid on each estate, by which the holder obtains an improper benefit. Evans, 216. See *Bankruptcy*, *Proof.*

DRAFT, see *Check.*

DRAWEE *of a bill of exchange*, is the person upon whom the bill is drawn, and is supposed to have effects of the drawer in his hands; after he has accepted the bill he is termed the acceptor. The drawee is the person from whom payment is to be regularly obtained, and the obligations of the other parties are a security for the bill being duly accepted and paid, provided the proper course is pursued by the holder.

DRAWER, *how he should subscribe his name.* The drawer of a bill should either subscribe his name at the bottom, or it should be inserted in the body of the instrument. Beawes' Pl. 3; Ld. Raym. 1376, 1542; and it must be written either by the person purporting to be the drawer or by some person by him authorised. If drawn or signed by an agent, it is usually signed in the following mode, "A B for C D," and if such agent do not express *for whom* he signs, he will be personally liable. And if signed by one person of a firm for himself and
partners,

partners, it is usual, and perhaps necessary to sign it as follows, " A B for A B and Company," or to that effect.

The bill or check should be completely *filled up* before the drawer signs his name to it, for if a person sign his name upon blank paper, stamped with a bill stamp, and deliver it to another to draw above the signature, he will be thereby bound to pay any sum which such stamp will carry. 1 H. B. 313.

D RAWER *of a bill, whether entitled to notice if the drawee have no effects.* If the drawer of a bill have no effects in the hands of the drawee, although it is said to be a settled point that he is not entitled to notice, it is nevertheless adviseable in the holder to give the regular notice, notwithstanding he is told that the drawee has no effects, for it is incumbent upon him to prove the truth of the fact, and not merely that such an answer was given. Walwyn *v.* St. Quentin. But see *Effects, Excuse for Notice.*

D RAWER, *the nature of his obligation.* The obligation of the drawer to pay is absolute and irrevocable; he is bound whether the bill be drawn on his own account or that of a third person, and upon the dishonour of the bill will
immediately,

immediately, before the time specified for payment in such bill, be liable to an action, not
only for the principal sum, but likewise, in
certain cases, for damages and interest, as a consequence of the bill not being honoured. 2 H. B.
379; Poth. Pl. 82. Exclusive of this obligation to the payee, he is further bound to indemnify the acceptor, if he should have no
effects in his hands, for any loss he may sustain
in consequence of his acceptance. Poth. Pl.
97, 98, 99. This obligation, although in its
nature absolute and irrevocable, may nevertheless be discharged by the laches or neglect of
the holder. See *Laches, Release, Waiver.*

E

EFFECTS. The holder of a bill accepted by a person having no effects does not relinquish his right against the drawer by taking security from the acceptor and giving him time. *Ex parte* Smith, 3 Bro. Ch. 1. Cooke's Bankrupt Laws.

EFFECTS, *how far the acceptor having no effects of the drawer will be an excuse for notice.* This very important question does not seem to have been distinctly settled, although from a case in the Common Pleas, Walwyn *v.* St. Quentin, 1 B. & P. 652, it has been inferred that in this case no notice is requisite. See this point more at large under the head *Excuse for Notice.*

L   EVIDENCE

EVIDENCE is that species of proof which the law requires from the party bringing his action, and it may be either *written* or *parol.* The evidence requisite must depend upon the nature of the action and the party against whom it is brought, whether as *acceptor, drawer, indorser, &c.* and it is a general rule that the best evidence shall be adduced which the nature of the case will admit.

EVIDENCE *in an action against the acceptor.* The plaintiff must in this case prove that the defendant accepted the bill either *verbally,* or in *writing;* if the latter, the *signature* must also be proved. The plaintiff must further prove the necessary *indorsements;* and if the acceptance was made *without sight,* the *signature of the drawer* must be also proved. If, however, the bill was accepted or indorsed *after sight,* the mere production of the instrument so accepted or indorsed will be sufficient evidence of the instrument's having been made, because such acceptance or indorsement admits the defendant's hand writing. 7 T. R. 604, 612. Upon this principle it has been held that even proof of the forgery of the drawer's hand writing is no defence for the acceptor or indorser in an action

action at the suit of a *bona fide* holder, if the defendant accepted or indorsed the bill *after* the subscription of the drawer's name. *Vide supra.* In an action by the drawer against the acceptor having paid the bill, it is not necessary to prove that the acceptor had effects of the drawer's in his hands. 10 Mod. 36, 37; 1 Wils. 185.

EVIDENCE *necessary if the bill was accepted by an agent.* The plaintiff must in this case prove that such agent or servant was legally authorized by his principal.

EVIDENCE *in an action against several acceptors.* The signature of each of the parties must be proved, Esp. Ca. N. P. 135; or that a partnership existed, and that the acceptance was made by one of them for himself and partners. Peake 16.

EVIDENCE *necessary in an action against the drawer or indorser of a bill or note.* The signature of the defendant, or his agent lawfully authorised—the necessary indorsements between him and the plaintiff—the presentment —the non-acceptance or non-payment—and the notice; and, in case of a foreign bill, the defendant must also prove a protest, as well as notice. If the bill were transferable by deli-

very

very only, the delivery must be proved: the plaintiff must also prove his interest in the bill, and how he became a party to it. The plaintiff must further prove that he used due diligence to obtain the money of the acceptor. Comyn 579. If the action be brought on the part of an indorser, having paid the bill, the plaintiff must prove that the instrument was returned to him, and that he paid it. Ld. Raym. 743. This should be proved by producing the bill with a receipt at the back of it. If it were an accommodation bill, and the acceptor sue the drawer, he must prove the hand writing of the defendant, and payment by himself, or something equivalent, such as his being in prison on a *capias ad satisfaciendum.*

EVIDENCE *necessary for payee in an instrument originally payable to bearer.* In this case the delivery of such bill to himself need only be proved, although, under suspicious circumstances, the plaintiff claiming as bearer only, and not as original payee, may be required to prove that he, or some person between him and the person who transferred it to him, took it *bona fide,* and gave a valuable consideration for it. Bayl. 116.

EVIDENCE

EVIDENCE *necessary to support the special count.* In proof of the allegation in the special count it is incumbent on the party to produce the instrument declared on, to prove that such instrument was *made.* In case of loss, however, it will be sufficient to produce a copy, or give parol evidence of its contents; but in either of these cases sufficient probability must be made appear to the Court, before the plaintiff will be admitted to read a copy, or give parol evidence of its contents. 1 Atk. 446.

EVIDENCE *if a bill is in possession of defendant.* In this case the plaintiff must give him notice to produce it, otherwise he will not be allowed to go into evidence of its loss or contents. Esp. 50; Peake 165.

EVIDENCE, *where the instrument itself will be proof.* In an action against the indorser or acceptor, where the bill was indorsed or accepted after it was complete, and *he had seen it,* the mere production of the instrument so by him accepted or indorsed will be sufficient evidence of its having been made, because such acceptance or indorsement admits the defendant's hand writing. 7 T. R. 604, 612. Upon this principle it has been adjudged, that even proof

of

of the forgery of the drawer's hand writing is no defence for the acceptor or indorser in an action at the suit of a *bona fide* holder, if the defendant accepted or indorsed the bill after the subscription of the drawer's name. 7 T. R. 604, 612.

EVIDENCE *of notice.* See *Notice.*

EVIDENCE *in case of a lost bill.* In an action against the drawer, confession that he made such bill was held sufficient. Hart *v.* King, 12 Mod. 309.

EVIDENCE *of protest.* See *Protest.*

EVIDENCE *parol.* See *Witnesses.* See also *Action, Declaration, Signature, &c.*

EXCHANGE is the difference in the value of money between two countries, and is dependent upon the relative abundance or scarcity of specie. If therefore any negotiation take place at Leghorn, where the merchants have large sums to remit to Marseilles and but little to draw from thence, there are more persons desirous of exchanging such bills for money. Consequently the want of bills upon Marseilles being greater than that of money, they are of more value (that is, the balance is in their favour *one* or *two* per cent. as the case may be,) and

you

you must pay a banker at Leghorn the amount of that balance in order to obtain such a bill; for instance, upon a balance of one per cent. 1010*l.* for a bill of 1000*l.*

The position that the price of exchange depends upon the relative scarcity or abundance of money, Mr. Evans observes was strikingly illustrated in the case of Hamburgh, about the latter end of the year 1799, where such large sums were due from Hamburgh to England, and so many bills dishonoured, and there was at the same time such a scarcity of cash to satisfy the holders of bills upon merchants in Hamburgh, that cash had risen to the price of near 20 per cent. and therefore, in order to obtain 100*l.* the amount which ought regularly to have been paid by the drawee in Hamburgh, a bill must have been given upon England for 120*l.*, and the person making the remittance was answerable to that extent, having his remedy over against all the antecedent parties. Evans 63.

EXCHANGE, *liability of the acceptor when the course has altered.* It is said by Poth. Pl. 174, that in a foreign bill where the course of exchange has altered the acceptor will only be

liable

liable according to the rate of such exchange when the bill became due.

EXCISE. In bills payable to the Excise it is customary to allow *six days*, exclusive of the three days of grace, upon paying one shilling to the clerks for their trouble; and it was held that this indulgence being universally known and allowed, the drawer was not discharged from his responsibility. Welfford *v.* Hawkins, Guildhall Sit. Hil. 1763; Esp. 59. Mr. Evans, however, doubts the principle of this decision, and conceives that the Commissioners of Excise have no more authority to introduce such a custom than the house of Messrs. Thellusson or any other mercantile house in the country.

EXCUSE *for notice, how far good, the drawer having no effects in the hands of the acceptor.* It has been laid down by some writers, that where the drawer has had no effects in the hands of the acceptor, that notice in this case may be dispensed with. This proposition has been laid down founded upon the case of Walwyn *v.* St. Quentin, 1 B. & P. 652. Upon this it is necessary to observe, that from this case, which was decided upon special circumstances, the inference has been drawn too generally. It is a general principle

principle that notice is, in almost every case, necessary, and it should be under very special circumstances indeed that such notice should be
dispensed with. Mr. Evans, after distinguish-
ing the case of Walwyn *v.* St. Quentin from
that of Bickerdike *v.* Bolman, (the principle of
which was that the drawer had no right to expect payment by the drawee in whose hands he
had no effects,) proceeds to observe, that to
every substantial purpose, as to the point in
question, the circumstance that a bill is drawn
for the benefit of the acceptor is equivalent to
the acceptor having effects of the drawer.

" Much prejudice might (Mr. Evans observes) under the circumstances of this case,
have resulted from the want of notice. At the
distance of several years after, the drawer (a
mere surety) had every reason to suppose the bill
satisfied either by the acceptor who had engaged
to pay it, or by the indorser, on whose account it
was to be paid, might be unexpectedly called
upon, and, by the death or bankruptcy of the
other parties, deprived of the opportunity of re-
dress; whereas, if immediate and regular notice
had been given, he might have taken up the bill
whilst he had the means of indemnifying himself.

self. If the holder of a bill is to be excused from pursuing the regular course prescribed by law on account of the equitable circumstances between the other parties, of which he has no cognizance, and with which he has no concern, these circumstances should at least be viewed in the aggregate, and applied to the principle which renders them material. Where a variation of the circumstances destroys the principle, on account of which the exception is introduced, the exception should not be allowed to continue. It is much more satisfactory to advert to the opinion given by the same respectable authority, Lord Chief Justice Eyre. " That as the guarantee was given in that mode, the legal consequences would follow so as to limit its generality, and that perhaps it would be better to adhere to the rule than to relax it."

Excuse *for notice, in what cases admissible.* The death of the holder, illness, or unavoidable accident, will be an excuse for notice, provided it be given as soon as possible after the impediment is removed; but notorious insolvency will be no excuse for not presenting a bill for payment to the person upon whom it is drawn.

drawn. 2 H. B. 609; nor is the holder of a negotiable instrument excused from making a protest, where such protest is necessary, and giving notice to the drawer and indorsers, although the notoriety of the failure of the drawee may appear to have given them sufficient information; for, as it is judiciously observed by a foreign jurist (Pothier), the formalities established by the laws to apprise persons of any fact cannot be dispensed with, and admit of no equivalent *(ne se supplent point, et ne s'accomplissent par équipollence)*.

Excuse *in case of death or illness*. See *Death, Illness*.

EXECUTION, *how far to be considered as a discharge*. If the holder of a bill or note obtain judgment in an action against any of the parties liable, and take any of the parties to such bill or note in execution, this will not operate in favour of any of the other parties, but will discharge that person only (1 **Wils**. 46, 115; 2 **Bla. R.** 1235; 4 T. R. 825;) for taking a person in execution is considered, as far as he is concerned, as a full satisfaction for the debt. 5 Co. 86.

Execution *against the goods*. Although the holder

holder of a bill may sue out executions against *the bodies* of all the parties, he nevertheless cannot issue a *fieri facias* to affect the *goods* of more than one. Stra. 515.

EXECUTOR. It is said that the executor of a deceased holder of a negotiable instrument may present it for payment, although he have not proved the will. See *Death*, *Presentment*.

EXPENCES *recoverable in case of dishonour of a negotiable instrument.* The only expence recoverable by the holder of a bill for its dishonour are those of noting and protesting, and therefore he cannot demand more of any of the parties to the bill than a satisfaction for that expence. But there are other incidental expences which one of the parties may have been obliged to pay to the holder in consequence of the refusal of the acceptor, such as *re-exchange*, *postage* and *commission*. 2 T. R. 52. For each of these see the respective heads. See also *Costs*, *Damages*, *Interest*, *Protest*, *Postage*, *Re-exchange*.

The above are the only legal charges, nor can any extraordinary expences which any of the parties may incur by travelling, or some advantageous engagement being delayed or defeated by by the want of punctual payment, be *legally* demanded in any possible case. Lex Mer. 461; Poth. Pl. 63.

EXPENCES *of proving under a commission of bankruptcy*. See *Bankruptcy*.

EXPENCES *of protest*. By 9 & 10 W. 3. c. 17, *sixpence only* is *allowed for protest* upon inland bills, although it is customary to *charge* more. See *Protest*.

EXTINGUISHMENT. If a person take a bill of exchange in satisfaction of a former debt, for which he has not a security of an higher nature than the bill, he will not be afterwards permitted to waive it, and sue the person from whom he received the bill for the original debt before the bill becomes due, because, under these circumstances, the receipt of the bill is an agreement to give credit to the person delivering the instrument for the length of time it has to run. Esp. Ca. N. P. 5, 106; 5 T. R. 513; Salk. 442; Skin. 416; Com. Dig. tit. Merchant, F. 17.

If however the person delivering such bill knew it to be of no value, it may be considered as a mere nullity, and the party sued may be taken a second time upon the same

M   writ,

writ, for the original debt. 12 Mod. 517;
6 & 7 T. R. 52, 64. See *Arrest*.

EXTINGUISHMENT *of right of action.* If the
holder of a bill make the acceptor his executor
and dies, the right of action against all the
parties is by this act extinguished. Poth. Pl.
191; 1 Rol. Ab. 922; Plowd. 184, 543;
2 Bla. Com. 511, 512; and if the holder of a
bill or note accept a bond from the drawer in
satisfaction of it, this will discharge the other
parties. 3 Mod. 87. See *Discharge, Satisfaction.*

F

FACTOR. If the factor of an Incorporate Company draw a bill on such Company, and one member accept it, this acceptance will not bind the Company, because it is a private act of the party, and not a public one of the Company; and upon this principle, if several persons, each acting in his individual capacity, employ one factor, who draws a bill upon all which is accepted but by one, such acceptance will not bind the rest. Bull. N. P. 279; Mar. 2. Ed. 16; Beawes' Pl. 228; Molloy, b. 2. c. 10. § 18. See *Agent, Partner.*

FEME COVERT, see *Married Women.*

FICTITIOUS NAMES. Bills payable to a fictitious

fictitious person, or his order, are in effect payable to bearer, and may be declared on as such against all the parties knowing such payee to have been a fictitious person.

Any person indorsing the fictitious name upon a bill to give it currency would be guilty of forgery. 3 T. R. 174, 182, 481; 1 H. B. 313, 569.

Any words in a bill, or extraneous facts, which might induce an inference that the person making a bill intended it to be negotiable, although payable to a fictitious payee, will give such bill a transferable quality.

FOREIGN BILLS, see *Bills of Exchange.*

FORGERY. The forgery of an indorsement in a bill transferable by indorsement only will convey no interest, and therefore any person getting possession of it by a forged indorsement will not acquire any interest in it, although he was not aware of the forgery, and consequently the original holder may in such case recover against the acceptor and drawer, although the acceptor may have paid the bill; and if the person attempting to derive an interest under such indorsement sues the acceptor, he will be admitted to prove that the indorse-

indorsement was not made by the person entitled to make it. 4 T. R. 28; 1 T. R. 607.

FORM *of a bill of exchange, promissory note, acceptance, indorsement, protest, &c.* See Appendix.

FRAUD, see *Over-due Bills.**

FUND. If a bill of exchange be made payable out of a particular fund, which possibly may not be productive, it will not, in the first instance, be negotiable; and there is considerable doubt whether it can become so by any subsequent circumstance. Kingston *v.* Long, B. R. M. 25 G. 3; Bayl. 8. acc. Lewis *v.* Orde. 1 Gilb. Evid. by Loft 179. *sembl. contra.*

————

GAMING, see *Considerations Illegal.*
GRACE, see *Days of Grace.*

* [A general intent to defraud is sufficient to constitute the crime. For if a person does such an act, the probable consequence of which is to defraud, that constitutes a fraudulent intent in the eye of the law. 3 T. R. 176.]

H

HOLDER. The holder of a bill of exchange is the person who is in possession of it
either by indorsement or delivery, or both, and
entitled to receive payment either from the
drawee or acceptor.*

HOLDER, *conduct he ought to pursue.* It is in
some cases necessary, and in all adviseable, unless the bill have been previously accepted, to
present it to the drawee for acceptance. If the
drawee refuse to accept, the holder ought, with
all possible dispatch, to give notice of such refusal to the various persons who became parties to the bill antecedent to himself.

Unless a bill be drawn payable within a specified time after sight, although it appears from
some

* [In England he is not considered as an assignee; *Secus,* in
Pennsylvania. Doug. 614. 4 Dall. 53.]

some authorities that it is not incumbent upon the holder to present a bill (unless payable after sight) before it is due, it is nevertheless, in all cases most adviseable to get it accepted as soon as possible, not only because another security is thereby added to the debtor, but because by acceptance only the person on whom the bill is drawn becomes debtor, and responsible to the holder. See *Notice, Presentment, Protest, &c.*

HOLDER, *how he should act in case of partial acceptance.* If upon presentment for acceptance the drawee has undertaken to pay a part, and the *holder* has given notice of such partial acceptance to the other parties, the holder, it is said, when such bill becomes due, should receive of the drawee the sum for which he accepted, and cause a protest to be made for non-payment of the sum remaining due. Mar. 68, 85, 86.

HOLDER, *his duty in case of loss,* see *Loss.* See also *Notice, Presentment, Protest, Acceptance, Indorsement, Transfer, &c.*

HONOUR, see *Acceptance for Honour.*

1

ILLEGAL CONSIDERATIONS. If a bill or note be given on an illegal consideration, or if it be fraudulently obtained, it is of no avail either to the original payee or to the person receiving it from him *with notice* of its original defect: and a late writer is of opinion, if the several persons through whose hands the instrument passes are all privy to the illegality of the original transactions, that such illegality will be a complete bar to the holder. But it has been decided in the case of Parr *v.* Elliason, East 92, that a person receiving a bill from an indorsee in the fair course of trade, and even *with notice* of the original illegality, shall be allowed to recover, for he succeeds to the rights

and

and privileges of the indorser, and these would be most unduly and unequitably restrained if he had not a complete power to transfer. See *Considerations Illegal.*

ILLNESS, *how far an excuse for notice.* Illness of the holder or his agent will be an excuse for the want of the regular notice of the dishonour of a negotiable instrument, provided such regular notice be given as soon as possible after the impediment is removed.

[INDEBITATUS ASSUMPSIT. Vid. Assumpsit.]

INDORSEMENT is that act by which the holder of a negotiable instrument transfers or assigns his right to another person, and this may be done either simply *by delivery*, where the instrument is payable *to bearer*, or by *indorsement and delivery* where it is payable *to order.*

Indorsements are of three species, viz. *in blank, in full,* and *restrictive.*

INDORSEMENT *in blank.* This is the most usual species of indorsement; it mentions no name, but the holder may write over it what name he pleases, and so long as it continues in blank it makes the instrument payable to bearer. And although it has been adjudged that such an indorsement does not transfer the property and interest in the instrument without some further

act,

act, it gives the indorsee, as well as any other person to whom it is afterwards transferred, the power of making himself assignee of the beneficial interest in the instrument, by filling it up payable to himself (as by writing over the indorser's name " pay the contents,") which may be done at the time of trial. 2 Str. 1103; 12 Mod. 244; 1 Salk. 127, 130; 1 Show. 163; Ld. Raym. 443; Comyn. 311; Barnes 453; Bull. N. P. 275, 278. As long as the first indorsement continues in blank, the instrument, as against the payee, drawer, and acceptor, is assignable by mere delivery, notwithstanding there may be upon it subsequent full indorsements.

INDORSEMENT *in full.* In this indorsement the name of the person in whose favour it is made is mentioned, and this indorsement may restrain the negotiability of the instrument.

INDORSEMENT *restrictive.* A restrictive indorsement has either express words which make it restrictive, or it is made in favour of a person incapable of making any further transfer. " Pay the contents to A. B. *only,*" is a restrictive indorsement. A restrictive indorsement precludes the person in whose favour it is
made

made from making a transfer so as to give a right of action either against the person making it, or any of the antecedent parties, or where such restriction is expressed upon the instrument, from retaining a payment to their prejudice. Archer *v.* Bank of England. The mere omission of words to give a power of transfer will not make an indorsement restrictive.

INDORSEMENT, *how to be made.* No form is required for an indorsement; it will be sufficient that the name of the indorser be written upon the back of the instrument, which is most usual, or any other part of it, either by the party making it or some other person duly authorized as his agent. An indorsement by a person not well known ought, in all cases, to state the place of his residence. Bull. N. P. 276.

INDORSEMENT *cannot be made for less than the full sum, unless part of it has been paid.* An indorsement cannot be made for less than the full sum appearing to be due upon the instrument transferred after it has been accepted, because a personal contract cannot be apportioned, and it would make the acceptor liable to two actions.

tions. Ld. Raym. 360; Carth. 366; 12 Mod. 213;
Salk. 65. If part of the bill however has been
paid, it may be indorsed over for the residue.
2 Wils. 262; 1 Salk. 65; Ld. Raym. 360;
Carth. 466; 12 Mod. 213.

INDORSEMENT *before time of payment mentioned, its operation.* Such an indorsement will
preclude the party making it from saying that
his indorsement was prior to the completion or
issuing of the bill or note, even against a person who knew at the time he took it in what
state the bill was at the time of the indorsement. Russel *v.* Langstaff, Doug. 496, 514.

INDORSEMENT *upon bills or notes for the
payment of less than 5l.* See *Small Notes.*

INDORSEMENT *if forged, in what cases it
will confer no title.* See *Forgery.*

INDORSEMENT *after bill or note becomes due.*
See *Fraud, Over-due Bills.*

INDORSEMENT, *how to be proved in evidence.*
The plaintiff claiming by indorsement should
prove the first indorsement by calling a witness
to prove the indorser's hand writing, in the
same manner as the acceptor's hand writing
must be proved. A confession of such signature has been held to be sufficient evidence
against

against the party making it. Cooper *v.* Le Blanc, Str. 1051; Ld. Raym. 742; but not against any other party. Hemmings *v.* Robinson, 1 Barnes, 317; and this will be sufficient if made pending a treaty for compromise. Waldridge *v.* Kunnison, Esp. 143. If the first indorsement was *in full*, the signature of the indorser must be proved; but if the first indorsement was *in blank*, it is not necessary to prove any of the subsequent indorsements, although they were in full; but in this case all the subsequent indorsements must be struck out at the time of the trial.

INDORSEMENT, *its legal obligation.* An indorsement implies an undertaking from the indorser to the person in whose favour it is made, and every other person to whom the bill or note may be afterwards transferred, exactly similar to that which is implied by drawing a bill, except that in the case of a note the stipulation with respect to the drawer's responsibility does not apply. A transfer by indorsement is an act similar to making a new bill in all its legal consequences, and the indorser may, in almost every respect, be considered as a new drawer on the original drawee; upon which principle

N   it

it has been decided, that a promissory note indorsed may be declared on as a bill of exchange. Str. 478; 1 Salk. 133; 3 Salk. 68; 2 Show. 441, 495, 501; 2 Burr. 674, &c. &c. A transfer by indorsement vests in the assignee a right of action on the bill against all the precedent parties to it.

INFANT, *his incapability of being party to a negotiable instrument.* No bill of exchange can properly be made or indorsed by an infant (in his own right), nor, as he is incapable of making himself responsible for the contract, properly addressed to him. Bayl. 24. Although, however, such contract by an infant is voidable, yet payment of such a bill to a minor, it is said, would be a valid payment (Poth. Pl. 166,) and an infant may sue for such payment. Poth. Pl. 166.

INLAND BILLS, see *Bills of Exchange.*

INSOLVENCY. The insolvency of the drawee or maker of a promissory note is no excuse for notice. See *Excuse, Notice.*

INSTALMENTS, *in what cases the whole amount is recoverable by the holder.* In a bill or note payable by instalments, where it contains a clause that on failure of payment of any one
instalment

instalment the whole shall become due, the holder is entitled to recover the whole amount of the several instalments; but where the instrument does not contain such a clause, it is doubtful whether the holder can legally take a verdict for more than the instalment due. According to the cases of Beckworth *v.* Nott, Rudder *v.* Price, 1 H. B. 551; and Cro. Jac. 565; Jenk. 333, the plaintiff is entitled to the *whole sum* for which the note was given; but according to other cases, particularly that of Ashford *v.* Hand, Andr. 370, the plaintiff is only entitled to the instalments due at the time of commencing the action. Where, however, all the instalments are due at the time of the trial, the Jury, for the sake of avoiding another action, will frequently give the full sum in damages.

INTENTION *of the parties to negotiable instruments.* Bills and notes are always so construed by Courts as to give them effect according to the intention of the contracting parties.

INTEREST, *from what time payable, and how to be computed.* A bill or note is generally understood to carry interest only from the time of the demand for payment, unless the delay

was

was occasioned by the defendant, as his being out of the kingdom at the time the instrument became due, 6 Mod. 138; Poth. Pl. 63, 64.

Interest is in some cases recoverable from the date of the instrument, D. Mar. 2d edit. 13. Blaney v. Bradley, Blackst. 761; but in general from the time when it would have been regularly payable down to the time when the plaintiff will be entitled to final judgment. Bayl. 91.

It was observed by Lord Mansfield, in the case of Robinson v. Bland, Burr. 1085, " that the general practice of the associates in taking damages in cases where the debt carried interest was, to stop *at the commencement of the action*, but that this practice was not founded in law, but in mistake and misapprehension; and that, in point of justice, interest should be carried down quite to the actual payment of the money. But as that could not be, it should be carried down to the time when the demand was completely liquidated *by the judgment being signed;* by which means complete justice was done to the plaintiff, and the temptation to a defendant to make use of all the unjust dilatories of chicane was taken away; for if interest were to stop at the commencement of
the

the suit, where the sum was large, the defendant might gain by protracting the cause in the most expensive and vexatious manner."

INTEREST, *how computed upon instruments payable on presentment.* Upon a bill or note payable on presentment interest must be computed from the presentment (Blaney *v.* Bradley); in which case the Court held that interest was due upon all bills of exchange and notes of hand payable at a day certain, or after demand if payable on demand. See also Bunb. 129; 2 T. R. 58.

INTEREST, *in what cases precluded.* A neglect to procure a protest upon any inland bill for the payment of 20*l.* upon which a protest might have been made, will, it is said, preclude the holder from recovering such interest from any person entitled to notice of the non-acceptance or non-payment of such instrument. 3 & 4 Anne, c. 9. § 5.

INTEREST upon *East India Bills.* See *Damage upon bills returned protested from India, p.* 76.

INTEREST *under a commission of bankruptcy.* The holder of a negotiable instrument is not entitled to any interest accrued or incurred after

the

the commission issued, nor where the act of bankruptcy to which the commission relates is ascertained, to any accrued or incurred after that act of bankruptcy. *Ex parte* Moore, 2 Bro. Cha. Ca. 597. See *Bankruptcy.*

INQUIRY. See *Judgment by default.*

I. O. U.—The common memorandum of I. O. U. has been decided not to amount to a promissory note. Esp. Ca. N. P. 426.

J

JOINT TRADERS, see *Partners*.

JUDGMENT BY DEFAULT. In cases of judgment by default it is now the practice of the Courts of King's Bench and Common Pleas to refer it to the Master to compute principal, interest, and costs. This however, has been refused to be adopted in the Court of Exchequer. 1 Anstr. Rep. 249, and in the other Courts it is still necessary to sue out a writ of inquiry, where the bill is payable in foreign money, the value of which can only be ascertained by a Jury. 4 T. R. 493; 5 T. R. 87; Tidd 485.

L

LACHES, see tit. *Neglect.*

LIABILITY *of the parties to negotiable instruments.* See *Obligation.*

LOSS *by the holder of a bill of exchange.* If the holder of a bill or check, transferable by mere *delivery*, loses it, and it comes to the hands of some person who was not aware of such loss for a good consideration, previous to its being due, such person, although deriving his interest in the instrument from the person finding it, may maintain his action against the acceptor, or other parties to the instrument, and the original holder, who lost it, will consequently forfeit all right of action. 12 Mod. 517; 3 T. R. 759; Holt 121; Ld. Raym. 738; Peacock *v.* Rhodes, Doug. 633.*

Loss,

* [This applies also to promissory notes. 1 Burr. 452. 3 Burr. 1516. 1524. 1 Bl. Rep. 485. 4 Bac. Abr. 705. 4 Dall. 51.]

Loss, *duty of the holder in this case.* The holder of a bill, whether transferable by delivery or not, ought, in all cases of loss, *immediately* to give notice of such accident to the acceptor and all the antecedent parties. Poth. Pl. 132; and if such bill were transferable by mere delivery, such holder should also give public notice of such loss, in order to prevent any person from taking it. Beawes' Pl. 179. It is said by Marius, that the holder of the bill which has been lost should, in the presence of a Notary and two witnesses, acquaint the acceptor with such loss, and signify to him that at his peril he pay it to none but himself or order. The same writer further observes, that no person should refuse to pay a bill to the loser which he has accepted, on the ground of its having been lost, if he have sufficient security and indemnification offered to him; and that if he should, under such circumstances, he will be liable to make good all losses, re-exchange, and charges. Marius 77, 80; Beawes' Pl. 182, 185; Vin. Ab. tit. Bills, R. Tercese *v.* Geray, Fin. Rep. 301.

Loss, *in what case the acceptor is bound to give another bill.* By 9 & 10 W. 3. c. 17. § 3, the holder

holder of a bill of above 5*l.* expressed for *value received*, and payable after date, may, in
case of loss, demand of the drawer another bill
of the same tenor with the original one, upon
giving security, and indemnifying him against
all persons whatsoever in case the lost bill
should again be found.

Loss *of one part of a foreign bill by the drawee.*
If one part of a foreign bill drawn in sets
should be lost by the drawee, he is bound to
give to the holder or his order a promissory
note for payment of the amount of the bill on
the day it becomes due, on delivery of the second part if it should arrive in time; if not,
upon the note, which is in all cases to have the
law and privileges of a bill of exchange: and
if the acceptor shall refuse to give such note,
the holder must protest immediately for non-
acceptance, and when due, must demand the
money, although he has neither the note nor
the bill, which, if refused, a protest must regularly be made for non-payment. Beawes' Pl.
188; Mar. 121; Bul. N. P. 271.

M

MARRIED WOMEN, *by whom a bill or note indorsed to them is to be transferred.* If a bill or note be made or indorsed to a fême sole, and she afterwards marry, the right of transfer vests in her husband, he being by the marriage entitled to all her personal property. 1 Str. 516; 3 Wils. 53; Sel. Ca. 96; 10 Mod. 246.

It is said by Pothier (Poth. Pl. 167), that payment to a married woman by a person knowing she was married will not discharge the person making it.

MARRIED WOMEN *their incapacity to become parties to bills of exchange.* See *Bills of Exchange,* p. 52.

MONTH,

MONTH, *how to be computed in negotiable instruments*. When bills are made payable at *one month*, or more after date, the computation must be by *calendar*, and not *lunar* months. Where one month is longer than that which precedes it, it is said to be a rule not to go into a third month in the computation. Thus on a bill dated 28th, 29th, 30th, or 31st of January, and payable one month after date, the time expires on the 28th of February in common years, and in the three latter cases, in leap-year, on the 29th. Chitty, 144, cites Mar. 75; Kyd 6.

N

NEGLECT to give notice of a bill's being dishonoured within a reasonable time, will discharge the parties from their respective obligations. Burr. 2670; 1 T. R. 712; Verito 45; Poth. Pl. 133. See *Notice.*

NEGLECT *of presentment.* If the holder of a bill neglect to present it to the drawee for payment at the time it becomes due, or, where no time is specified, within a *reasonable time* after the receipt of the instrument, he shall not afterwards resort to the drawer or indorsers, whose contracts are collateral only to pay in default of payment by the drawee, and not immediate or absolute, and who are always

O   presumed

presumed to have sustained damage by the holder's laches. 2 Burn. 669; 7 T. R. 581.

NEGLECT *of presentment or notice, occasioned by the sudden death or illness of the holder or his agent.* See *Death, Excuse, Illness.*

NEGOTIABILITY. It is not essential to the validity of a bill as an instrument that it should be transferable from one person to another. 6 T. R. 123; 7 T. R. 243. Smallwood *v.* Rolfe, Sel. Ca. 18. If, however, it be intended to be made negotiable, the operative words of transfer should always be inserted therein; for unless a bill contain some words empowering the proprietor to assign it, it cannot be transferred so as to give the assignee a right of action against any of the parties to the instrument except the assigner. 1 Salk. 133. Any words, however, or extraneous facts, from whence it can be inferred that the party making the instrument intended it to be negotiable, will give it a transferable quality as against *him;* and though no words are to be found upon the instrument authorising a transfer, yet it will always have the same effect against the party making it as if he had power to assign. The usual modes of making a bill transferable are,

by

by drawing it either payable to A. B. *or order*, or to A. B. or *his assigns*, or to A. B. *or bearer*, or to the drawer's own order.

NON-ACCEPTANCE, or NON-PAY-MENT, *to whom notice must be in these cases given.* See tit. *Notice, Protest, &c.*

NOTARY PUBLIC, see *Noting, Protest.* For his Fees of Office, see Appendix.

NOTES, see *Cash Notes, Bank Notes, Promissory Notes, Small Notes.*

NOTICE is that information which the holder of a negotiable instrument is bound to give to all the antecedent parties if the drawee refuse to accept, or, having accepted, if he refuse payment, or if he offer an acceptance varying from the tenor of the bill; in either of the above cases the bill is dishonoured, and the holder, in case of neglect to communicate notice within a reasonable time, will not be at liberty to resort to the other parties, who by such negligence will be discharged from their respective obligations. Burr. 2670; 1 T. R. 712; Ventr. 45; Poth. Pl. 133. The right of the drawer or indorsers to receive notice in case of the bill's being dishonoured is so strong a principle of law, and in all cases so indispensable,

able, that nothing but what has been by the act of God rendered impossible, can be an excuse for the want of it, unless, indeed, in those particular cases where the parties who would otherwise have been entitled have by their own act incapacitated themselves to insist upon the want of it. It is not material *who* informs the drawer of non-acceptance or non-payment of the bill, because notice is merely required that he may have recourse to the acceptor. Shaw *v.* Croft, cor. Ld. Kenyon, Sit. after Trin. 1798.

NOTICE *of conditional or partial acceptance* should be given to the other parties to the bill by the holder, on default of payment; for if under these circumstances a general notice of non-acceptance to any of the parties omitting to mention in such notice the *nature of the acceptance offered*, the acceptor is discharged by this act of the holder from his acceptance. 1 T. R. 182.

NOTICE *in case of foreign bills.* Wherever a notice is requisite in case of dishonour of foreign bills, a protest is also necessary, and notice of non-acceptance should be transmitted *within a reasonable time* after protest, to all the
                                    parties

parties to whom he means to resort, 2 H. B. 569; nor must the holder delay giving notice till the bill is protested also for non-payment. 1 Bul. N. P. 271. It is not necessary that a copy of the protest should accompany the notice of non-acceptance, Esp. Ca. N. P. 511, 512; Bul. N. P. 271; nor is it necessary to send the protested bill; Mar. 98; but a notice of the protest is in all cases necessary. 12 Mod. 309; Ventr. 45.

NOTICE *in case of foreign bills, when to be given.* Notice should be given on the day of refusal to accept, if any post or ordinary conveyance sets out on that day, and if not, by the next earliest ordinary conveyance. 4 T. R. 174; Ld. Raym. 743; 2 Str. 829; Mar. 97. Sending by the post, both in foreign and inland bills, will be sufficient, even though the letter should miscarry, and where there is no post, it will be sufficient to send notice by the *ordinary* mode of conveyance, *although it may not be the earliest.* 2 H. B. 565.

NOTICE *in case of inland bills, when to be given.* In inland bills not protested for non-acceptance, *if the parties reside in the same place* where the bill was dishonoured, notice should be given

on

on the same day, if possible, and by *that day's post* if the parties are resident out of that place. In inland bills protested for non-acceptance, if the notice or protest thereof are not sent *within fourteen days after it is made*, the drawer or indorser will not be liable for damages, &c. 3 & 4 Anne, c. 9. § 5. Notice should be given by the holder to the person from whom the bill was received, and although such notice may enure to the benefit of all the antecedent parties, and thereby make any further notice unnecessary, it is nevertheless adviseable for every party, *immediately upon the receipt of such notice*, to give a *fresh one* to such of those persons as are liable over to him, and against whom he must prove notice. Bayl. 83.

NOTICE, *how to be given if the person entitled to it be abroad.* Notice of non-acceptance should be left in this case at the place of his residence in England, if he have one, and payment demanded of his wife or servant. Esp. Ca. N. P. 511, 512. See *Presentment in case of Removal.*

NOTICE, *its operation in case of bills accepted after due.* If a bill be accepted after it become due, if notice have been given *at the time the bill became due,* of non-acceptance or non-payment,
the

the acceptor will be bound to pay such bill on *demand,* the drawer and indorser being by such notice still held liable. 12 Mod. 410; Ld. Raym. 364, 574; Beawes' Pl. 224.

NOTICE *reasonable, by whom to be decided.* This is partly a question of *fact,* and *partly of law,* dependent in some degree upon facts, such as, the distance at which the parties reside from each other, the course of the post, &c. but when these facts are once established, *the reasonableness of the time becomes a question of law for the determination of the Court. Sed qu.?* Per Ld. Mansf. and Buller, in Tindal *v.* Brown, 1 T. R. 168; Doug. 514, *contra.* *

NOTICE *in case of bankruptcy of the drawer.* Such notice not having been given to a person accepting a bill after such bankruptcy, he will be justified in paying such acceptance, although he has afterwards heard of such bankruptcy. 7 T. R. 711. See *Bankruptcy.*

NOTICE *in case of loss,* see *Loss.*

NOTICE *of discharge of servant,* see *Servant.*

NOTICE *of dissolution of partnership,* see *Partnership.*

* [In Pennsylvania the question of reasonable notice is entirely a question of fact, for the jury to determine. 4 Dall. 129.]

O

OBLIGATION *of parties to negotiable instru-ments.* See the respective heads *Acceptance, Drawer, Indorsement, Holder, &c.*

ORDER. Bills payable to order are assign-able by indorsement and delivery only. See *Delivery, Indorsement.*

OVER-DUE BILLS. A bill or note over due carries with it circumstances of suspicion which do not attach upon bills transferred in the regular course, where the transfer carries no suspicion upon the face of it, and the as-signee receives it on its own intrinsic credit, without being bound to enquire into any cir-cumstances existing between the assignee and any of the previous parties to the bill, as he will

not

not be affected by any of these transactions.
Per Bull. J. 3 T. R. 82. In a transfer, however, of a negotiable instrument *after due*, the
assignee receives it subject to all the legal as
well as equitable interests existing between the
antecedent parties to the instrument of which
he was aware at the time of the transfer.—
This mode being out of the common course of
dealing, affords ground for suspicion, in consequence of which it is always left to the Jury,
on the slightest circumstance, to presume that
the indorsee was acquainted with the facts
rendering the transaction unfair. 3 T. R. 83.
Where the bill was *noted before it was transferred* this circumstance was held sufficient ground
to presume that the indorsee was acquainted
with the impropriety of the transfer, *vid. sup.*
and the mere circumstance of a bill's having
been over due, has been expressed to be sufficient ground for a Jury to presume a knowledge of fraud in the assignee. 7 T. R. 430. It
has, however, been said that fraud is not to be
presumed without further evidence, although
that evidence need not amount to demonstration.
Castle *v.* Davies, cor. Ld. Kenyon, Sit. G. H.
16 Feb. 1796; 3 T. R. 83; 1 Wils. 230.

It

It has been decided that a party to a negotiable instrument transferring it to another person after it became due, shall not be at liberty to object to the payment of it when in the hands of a third person, who must necessarily also have received it after it was due; because, as payment could not have been demanded when the instrument was due, as it was not then issued, the difficulty was occasioned by the party himself who so put it into an improper circulation. Chitty, 114, 115.

P

PAROL ACCEPTANCE. See *Acceptance Verbal.*

PARTIAL PAYMENT. Whether if the holder, upon presentment of a negotiable instrument, accepting payment *of a part* in satisfaction, without the assent of the other parties to a bill, shall exonerate these parties, is a point not yet *completely* decided. It is the generally received opinion that this being the election of the holder to receive payment from the acceptor, the other parties are consequently discharged, although the holder has given regular notice of this partial dishonour. It has however been said, and that by two writers of considerable authority, that if a bill regularly accepted

cepted be presented for payment, and the whole sum is not paid, the holder may receive part in payment; and if he immediately protests for non-payment of the residue, such partial receipt will not release the obligation of the other parties with respect to the residue, because having obtained part of the money is in favour of those parties. Bull. N. P. 271, 273, 275; Mar. 36.

Receiving part from the acceptor of the instrument will in no case discharge the drawer if the bill was for accommodation only (Cooke 167), and if the holder of an accommodation bill receive a part from the drawer, and take a promise from him upon the back of the bill for payment of the residue at an enlarged time, it may become doubtful whether such act will discharge the acceptor. Ellis *v.* Gallindo, cited Doug. 250; Bayley 55. acc. 1 H. B. 88. *semb. cont.* See Appendix. *

PARTIAL ACCEPTANCE. see tit. *Acceptance, Indorsement, Transfer.*

PARTIES *to negotiable instruments.* Any persons may become parties to negotiable instruments who are capable of binding themselves by a contract. See the several titles

Bills,

---

* [Taking a note for goods sold is a payment, because it was part of the original contract; but paper is no payment where there is a precedent debt. Ld. Raym. 930. Chitty 122, 3. 7 T. R. 65, 6.]

*Bills, Checks, Notes, Drawee, Acceptor, In-
dorser, Holder, Infants, Married Women, &c.*

PARTNERS. Where there are two joint
traders and one accepts a bill for himself and
partner drawn on both, both will be bound if
it concern the trade. It has been said, indeed,
that the act of one partner will not bind the
other if it concern him only in a distinct interest. 1 Salk. 125. By more recent authorities, however, this appears to be contradicted,
for it was decided in the case of Sheriff *v.*
Wilkes, that the act of one partner in the name
of the firm is obligatory upon the others though
it may be on his own separate account, unless
the parties claiming the benefit of it received it
with knowledge of that circumstance; in which
case the others will not be bound. Sheriff *v.*
Wilkes, East 48. See also Peake 80; 2 Vern.
277, 292; Esp. 524; and one partner may
pledge the credit of his co-partner to any
amount by any act in the way of merchandize
done in the name of the firm, or of all the parties. Burr. 1216, 1221; 1 Bla. Rep. 295.
One partner, however, cannot bind another *by
deed* without his express authority. 1 T. R.
313; 7 T. R. 207.

PARTNER.

PARTNER. If a bill be drawn by two persons who are not partners, payable to their order, it must be indorsed by both. 1 Bla. Rep. 295.

PARTNERS, *how far an authority to one to act for all will be binding upon the firm.* An express authority given by several partners to one to act for all of them, empowers the party so authorised to act in the double capacity of agent and partner; but his power and authority being *express*, he must be guided by it. An authority given to one partner to receive all debts owing to, and to pay all debts due from a partnership on its dissolution, does not authorise such party to indorse a bill of exchange in the name of the partnership, though drawn by him in that name and accepted by a debtor of the partnership after the dissolution. Kilgour *v.* Finlayson, 1 H. B. 155.

PARTNERS, *how bills should be accepted by them.* If a bill be accepted by one partner only on the partnership account, he should subscribe the name of the firm, or express that he accepts for himself and partner. 1 Salk. 126; Ld. Raym. 175; Carvick *v.* Vickery, Doug. 653; Ld. Raym. 1484.

The right of transfer in copartnerships is
in

in all collectively, and not in any one individually, although with respect to the mode of transfer the right of several persons when in partnership, may be put in force by the indorsement of one partner only, in which case the transfer is considered as made by all the persons entitled to make it. *Vide supra.*

PARTNERSHIP, *limitation with respect to number*. By 6 Anne, c. 22. § 9, and G. 2. c. 13. § 13, no co-partnership exceeding the number of six persons (the Governor and Company of the Bank of England excepted) shall borrow, owe, or take up any sum or sums of money on their bills or notes payable on demand, or at any less time than six months from the borrowing thereof.

PARTNERSHIP, *notice of dissolution, how to be given*. This should not only be given in the Gazette, as is the usual practice, but it must be brought home to the knowledge of the holder of any negotiable instrument in which the firm is concerned; under these circumstances, therefore, it is incumbent upon the partners *to give notice to all their individual correspondents;* otherwise, notwithstanding the notice in the Gazette, they will stand responsible

sible for all bills negotiated by one of the former partners in the name of the firm.

PAYEE, *how to be described in a bill.* Unless the payee be properly described in a negotiable instrument, it is said that it will be mere waste paper. 1 H. B. 608. Care should be taken that the name of the payee should be properly spelled (Beawes' Pl. 3); and where there are two persons, the payee should be so described that no mistake can arise with respect to his personal identity. 4 T. R. 28.

PAYEE *of bills, under five pounds,* see *Small Notes.*

PAYMENT *of bills, checks, or notes, its operation.* The contract of the parties to a negotiable instrument is terminated upon the payment, at least so far as to prevent their being subject to new engagements; no indorsement, therefore, can be made after payment so as to affect the parties making it; and in an action where it appeared that the drawer had paid the bill and indorsed it over to the plaintiff, it was decided that such indorsement could not vest in the plaintiff any right of action against the acceptor. A person, however, not originally a party to a bill, by paying it *for the honour* of the

parties

parties to it, acquires a right of action against all the parties. Esp. 112. and after payment of a part only, a bill or check may be indorsed over for the residue. Ld. Raym. 360.

PAYMENT *after revocation of indorsement.* See *Revocation of Indorsement.*

PAYMENT *under misapprehension of facts.*— The payment of a bill or note under misapprehension of facts, or of the law arising out of them, which the party making the payment was under no legal obligation to discharge, as when the person whom he had paid had been guilty of laches, which might have been a sufficient ground of defence if the bill had not been paid, may be recovered back in an action for money had and received to the use of the plaintiff. Chatfield *v.* Paxton and Co. Sittings after Tr. T. 38 G. 3.

PAYMENT *by and to whom to be made.* Payment of a bill may not only be made by the acceptor but also by any other party, and even by a total stranger, as in the case of payment supra protest, Poth. Pl. and payment by the bail of either of the parties. 1 Wils. 46. Payment should be made to the real proprietor of the instrument, or his agent lawfully appointed

and

and empowered to receive it; for if he has ceased to be proprietor from having indorsed it to some other person, it will not be valid. Poth. Pl. 164.

PAYMENT *within what time to be made.*— Where a day certain is appointed it is a general rule that the party bound shall be allowed till *the last moment* of the day to pay it in, if it be an inland bill. 1 Rol. Rep. 189; 1 Saund. 287; 4 T. R. 173. It does not appear to be settled whether the acceptor has not the whole day for payment of an inland bill. 4 T. R. 170. With respect to foreign bills, the case is different, for as the protest upon a foreign bill should be made upon the last day of grace, so as to be sent, if possible, by the post on that day, it follows that the holder may insist on payment *on demand* on the last day of grace, or at least before the hours of business are expired. 1 Ld. Raym. 743.

PAYMENT *of part, how far to be considered as a discharge,* see *Waiver of Acceptance.*

PAYMENT *of part in accommodation bills,* see *Accommodation Bills, p.* 17.

PAYMENT *in case of bankruptcy, death, infants, married women, loss, robbery, &c.* see the respective heads.

PAYMENT

PAYMENT *of debt and costs*, see *Costs*.

PLACE *where the bill is made*. This should be superscribed upon the instrument, and where the maker is not a person well known in the commercial world, it is adviseable for him to mention *the number of the house and the street* where he resides, that the holder may be better enabled to find him out in case his responsibility be doubtful, or in case acceptance and payment are refused by the drawee. By the Small Note Bill, 17 G. 3. c. 30, in bills under five pounds this is absolutely essential to the validity of the instrument. See *Small Notes*.

PLEAS, see *Defence*.

POST. Sending notice by the post in case of the dishonour of a foreign or inland bill of exchange, will be sufficient, even though the letter should miscarry. 2 H. B. 509. acc. Barn. Rep. B. R. 199.

PRESENTMENT *for payment, by whom to be made*. This should in general be made by the holder, or his agent, being competent to give a legal discharge for the same to the person in general upon whom it is drawn. 1 Esp. 115; Poth. Pl. 129; and notwithstanding former doubts upon this subject, a person a person in possession of a bill payable to *his own order* is a sufficient holder for this purpose. 10 Mod. The demand for payment need not be personal, it will be sufficient if it be made at the place appointed by the party for payment, or of his agent who has been accustomed to pay money for him; but presentment for and demand of payment should be made on the person, and at the place appointed, if made or accepted by such person, at such particular place, or by a particular person not party to the instrument. Esp. 512; 2 H. B. 509; 12 Mod. 241. In default of the above, the acceptor and the other parties would in general be discharged from their obligations.

PRESENTMENT *second, when unnecessary.* If presentment be made, and payment refused, although in general, notice must be given, yet it will be unnecessary to make another presentment to the acceptor in person, the contract being in this case broken. Mar. 106; 2 H. B. 509; Com. Dig. tit. Merchant, F. 7.

Although the person at whose house the instrument is made payable is not a party to it, and consequently not personally liable, yet an answer by him, or at his house, as to the payment

ment or non-payment of it, will be sufficient. Esp. 4. If the person at whose house the bill is made payable is himself the holder of it, it is a sufficient demand of payment for such person to inspect his books, and sufficient evidence of a refusal to find upon such inspection that he has no effects in his hands. 2 H. B. 309. See *Evidence, Demand, Presentment.*

PRESENTMENT *in case of death, removal, &c.* If the drawee or acceptor be removed from the place where the bill was originally made payable, the holder should endeavour to find him out, and there present it: if he have absconded, no further enquiry becomes necessary; if he have left the country, presentment and demand of payment of his wife or agent, at the place where he formerly resided, will be sufficient. Collins *v.* Butler, Str. 1687; Ld. Raym. 743; Esp. 511. If the drawee be dead, the bill should be presented for payment to his personal representative; and if there should be none, payment should be demanded at the house of the deceased; and if the deceased have no widow nor presumptive heirs, Pothier is of opinion that the holder will in this case be excused from making any protest. A late writer,

writer, however, (Mr. Evans,) observes most judiciously, " that a presentment at the house where a negotiable instrument is made payable will be sufficient if the drawee be dead, and that the collateral enquiries ought to fall *not* upon the holder, but the indorser, and finally upon the drawer, who have all engaged for payment *at that place*. If no place of payment be expressed, and the drawee be dead, application should be made at his last dwelling house; and the bill not being paid there, should be taken up by the anterior parties without subjecting the holder to search for the personal representative. See *Death, Removal of the Acceptor.*

PRESENTMENT *for payment, within what time to be made*. This must in all cases be done within a reasonable time; and there is some doubt whether what shall be a *reasonable time* should be a question of fact for the determination of a Jury, or a question of law for the decision of the Court. Upon a bill or note payable upon demand or at sight, in London, in one case a presentment the next morning after its receipt was held sufficiently early, a presentment at *two* the next afternoon too late. Ward *v.* Evans, Ld.

Ld. Raym. 928; East India Company *v.* Chittey, Str. 1175. In a later case, however, where a similar note was given in London at *one,* but not presented till the next morning, two Juries held this delay unreasonable, but the Court was of a contrary opinion. Appleton *v.* Sweetapple, B. R. M. 23 G. 3.

Bills or notes should be presented for payment upon the last day of grace, and within a reasonable time before the expiration of that day; negotiable instruments should also be presented within *seasonable hours* or *hours of business:* thus if by the known custom of any place bills are only payable within limited hours, a presentment *there* out of such hours is unseasonable; and so is a presentment out of the hours of business to a person of any particular description in any place where by the known custom of such place all persons of his description begin and leave off business at certain stated hours.

PRESENTMENT *for payment by a banker.* Bills or notes paid into the hands of a banker must be presented by him as soon as if it had been paid into his hands by a customer; and such instrument, if payable where the banker resides,

sides, must be presented the next time the banker's clerk goes his usual rounds. Hankey *v.* Trotman, Bl. 1.

PRESENTMENT, *what delays in are admissible,* see *Delay, p.* 94.

PROOF, see *Dividend.*

PROMISE. In the case of Mason *v.* Hunt it was laid down by Lord Mansfield, that if one man to give credit to another make an *absolute promise* to accept his bill, the drawer, or any other person, may shew such promise upon the Exchange to get credit, and a third person who should advance his money upon it would have nothing to do with the equitable circumstances which might subsist between the drawer and the acceptor. In a subsequent case, however, that of Johnson *v.* Collings, East 98, Mr. Justice Le Blanc having added the preceding extract from Lord Mansfield's opinion, Lord Kenyon said he thought that the admitting a promise to accept before the existence of a bill, to operate as an absolute acceptance afterwards, even with the qualification of credit being given by a third person upon the faith of such an assurance, was carrying the doctrine of implied acceptance to the utmost verge of the

the law, and he doubted *whether it did not even go beyond it.*

PROMISE *to accept in future,* whether made to the drawer or not, as a promise contained in a letter to accept such bills as the plaintiff should draw on the defendant at a future day, on account of a debt due from a third person to the plaintiff, will operate against the person making it as an absolute acceptance. 3 Burr. 1663, 1672; Cowp. 571.

PROMISE *upon an executory consideration, how far binding.* A promise upon an executory consideration will not bind as long as such consideration remains executory, unless it influences some person to take or to retain the bill. Bayl. 49; and if the promise to accept in future be obtained by fraud, it shall in no case be binding. Burr. 1669.

PROMISSORY NOTES. A promissory note is a written promise for payment of a specific sum of money at a certain time, deriving its existence and privileges from the 3d & 4th Anne, c. 9. The person who subscribes the note is called the maker, the other parties are the same as those to bills of exchange; and these instruments are placed by the statute,

Q   with

with respect to *time* when payable, days of grace, and mode of payment, precisely upon the same footing as bills of exchange.

In the case of Heylin *v.* Adamson, Lord Mansfield observed, that " although while a promissory note continues in its original shape of a promise from one man to another it bears no similitude to a bill of exchange, yet when it is indorsed the resemblance begins, for then it is an order by the indorser upon the maker of the note to pay to the indorsee; the indorser becomes as it were the drawer; the maker of the note, the acceptor, and the indorsee, the payee. The above point of resemblance once fixed, the law relative to bills becomes equally applicable to promissory notes." See *Stamps, Bills of Exchange, Presentment, Protests, &c.*

PROOF, see tit. *Evidence.*

PROTEST is a minute of non-acceptance or non-payment of a bill of exchange, and a solemn declaration on the part of the holder against any loss to be sustained from the non-acceptance or non-payment of a bill of exchange.

PROTEST *upon foreign bills.* In all cases of the dishonour of a foreign bill where notice is necessary,

necessary, a protest must be made, which, although matter of form, is nevertheless, by the custom of merchants, indispensable, and it is said to be part of the constitution of a foreign bill. Ld. Raym. 993; 6 Mod. 8; 2 T. R. 713; 5 T. R. 239; Holt 121.

PROTEST *upon foreign bills, how to be made.* The holder, or his friend (if he is ill or absent) in case of non-acceptance or non-payment of a foreign bill, should carry it to a notary, who is to present it to the drawee and again demand acceptance; which if refused, the notary is there to make a minute on the bill itself, consisting of his initials, the month, day, and year, and the reason (if any assigned) for non-acceptance, together with his charges for making such minute. After this, a solemn declaration is to be drawn up by the notary (upon the bill itself, if it can be had, if not, upon a copy), that the bill has been presented for acceptance, which was refused, and that the holder intends to recover all damages which he, or his principal, or any other party may sustain on account of the non-acceptance. Poth. Pl. 134; Mal. 264; Mar. 16. The minute is termed the *noting*, and the solemn declaration the *protest*, to which all fo-

reign

reign Courts give credit. Molloy 281; Skin. 272. pl. 1; 2 Bac. Ab. new edit. 725. The want of a protest can in no case be supplied by noting, which is a mere preparatory minute of which the law of England takes no cognizance as distinguished from the protest. See *Noting*.

PROTEST *where no notary*. Bills are protested in this country, if there be no notary resident at or near the place where payable, by some substantial resident, in the presence of two or more witnesses, between sun-rise and sun-set, and should in general be made at the place where payment is refused; but when a bill is drawn abroad, directed to the drawee at Southampton, or any other place, requesting him to pay to the payee in London, the protest for non-acceptance of such bill may be made either at Southampton or London. Chitty 92, cites Mar. 107.

PROTEST *its form*. The form of a protest must always be conformable to the custom of the country where it is made, Poth. Pl. 155; and a copy of the bill must be prefixed to all protests, with the indorsements transcribed *verbatim*, with an account of the reasons given by the party why he does not honour the bill.

Mar.

Mar. 107. and to be received in evidence, it must be written on paper stamped with a two-shilling stamp. 37 G. 3. c. 90. It has been recently decided that it is not necessary that a copy of the protest should accompany the notice of non-acceptance, neither is it necessary to send the protested bill, but a copy of the protest should in all cases be given. Esp. Ca. N. P. 511, 512; Bull. N. P. 271; Mar. 68, 86, 87, 120; Lov. 100; 12 Mod. 309; Vent. 45.

PROTEST *upon foreign bills, within what time to be made.* No adjudication, it is said, has been yet made with respect to this point, but from analogy with respect to the time when such protest should be made for non-payment, it should be made in this country within the usual hours of business, on the day when acceptance is refused. Mar. 112; 4 T. R. 174.

PROTEST *upon inland bills.* By 3 & 4 Anne, c. 9. § 4, a protest *may be made* for an inland bill, if such bill be for the payment of 5*l.* or upwards, within a limited time after date, and the value expressed to have been received, or after an acceptance written on such bill for its non-payment; but a protest cannot properly

be made on any other inland bills. See also
9 & 10 W. 3. c. 17. § 1. But a protest upon
an inland bill is never necessary where the bill
is for payment of less than 20*l.*; and in such as
are for more, a neglect to procure it will only
preclude the holder from recovering against the
persons entitled to notice, and special damages
or costs occasioned by the non-acceptance, non-
payment, and interest. 3 & 4 Anne, c. 9. § 6.
Brough *v.* Parkins, Ld. Raym. 992; Str. 910.
If the bill, however, be under 20*l.* it does not
appear to have been decided whether the holder
would not be entitled to the above as an accu-
mulative remedy, although no protest was made.
9 & 10 W. 3. c. 17. § 6. A protest upon inland bills, however, is very unusual in practice,
such bills being only *noted for non-acceptance.*

For abstracts of the above cited statutes, see
Appendix.

PROVISION, see *Commission, Discount.*

R

RECEIPT. The receipt of a bill or note need not, like other receipts, be stamped; it is usually given on the back of the bill. A general receipt on the back of the bill is *prima facie* evidence of its having been paid by the acceptor (Peake 25), and therefore it is in all cases adviseable, where payment is made by a drawer or indorser, to state in the receipt that it was made by him, because he will not in such case be put to the trouble of proving payment by a witness. In a case reported by Ld. Raym. 742, a plaintiff was non-suited because he could not produce a receipt for the money paid by him to the indorsee upon the protest, according to the custom of merchants, although

Judge

Judge Holt seemed to be of opinion in that case that if the plaintiff could have adduced any evidence of the bill's having been paid, it would have been sufficient.

RE-EXCHANGE is the expence incurred by the bill's being dishonoured in a foreign country where it is made payable, and returned back to that country in which it was made or indorsed, and there taken up; the amount of this depends upon the course of exchange between the two countries through which the bill has been negotiated. In other words, re-exchange is the difference between the draft and the re-draft. When a bill is drawn upon a foreign country the first thing that should be enquired into is, the value of money in that country. If, for example, a bill be drawn payable in France, and there dishonoured, if the rate of exchange should at such period of its dishonour be in favour of France, and the bill is returned to this country, and the drawer or indorser is called upon to take it up, he may, as actually happened in the case of Mellish *v.* Simeon, (see this case in the Appendix,) be obliged to pay 309*l.* 4*s.* 5*d.* more than the amount of the bill. The drawer of a bill is liable for the whole amount of the re-exchange

exchange occasioned by the circuitous mode of returning the bill through the various countries in which it has been negotiated, as much as for that occasioned by a direct return, although payment of the bill was expressly prohibited by the laws of the country where it was drawn.

RE-EXCHANGE *upon Indian or American bills,* see *Damages,* p. 76.

REFERENCE *to the Master,* see *Judgment by Default, Writ of Inquiry.*

RE-ISSUING *bills or notes,* see Appendix.

RELEASE. What amounts to an assent to discharge an acceptor has been held by the Courts to be a question for the Jury arising out of the circumstances of the case. Ellis *v.* Galindo, cited in Dingwall *v.* Dunster, Doug. 247, (see these cases in the Appendix.) In the last case it was held that nothing but an express consent or the statute of limitation would discharge the acceptor. Doug. 247; Anderson *v.* Cleland, Esp. N. P. 46. If the holder give a release to the drawee after the bill is drawn, and before acceptance, this will not discharge him from the obligation raised by a subsequent acceptance, because he was not chargeable at the time of such release. Ld. Raym. 65. See *Discharge, Satisfaction, Waiver.*

REMOVAL

REMOVAL *of the acceptor*, see *Absconding*, *Presentment in case of removal.*

REMEDY *in case of non-payment of a negotiable instrument*, see *Action, Bankruptcy. &c.*

ROBBERY *if a negotiable instrument be stolen or lost*, see *Loss.*

S

SATISFACTION, see *Discharge, Execution, Extinguishment, Payment.*

SERVANT. If a bill be drawn upon a man by the description of a servant, a general acceptance will bind him personally. Thomas *v.* Bishop, Anne 1 Str. 955. See *Agent, Signature.*

SETS. Foreign bills generally consist of several which are called sets, each part of which contains a condition that it shall be payable only so long as the others remain unpaid; in every other respect they are all counterparts of each other.

In bills drawn in sets the condition should be inserted in each part, and should mention in each

each every *other part* of the set: for if a person having the intention to make a set of three parts should omit the condition in the first, and make the second with a condition mentioning the first only, and in the third take notice of the other two, he might perhaps be in some cases obliged to pay each; for it would be no defence to an action on the second that he had paid the third, nor to an action on the first that he had paid either of the others.

Where a bill consists of several parts, each ought to be delivered to the person in whose favour it is made, unless one be forwarded to the drawee for acceptance, in which case the rest must be also so delivered, otherwise difficulties may occur in negotiating the bill or obtaining payment. Bayl. 15.

SIGNATURE *to a bill of Exchange.* The name of the drawer of a bill of exchange should be either subscribed at the bottom, or inserted in the body of it. Beawes' Pl. 3; Ld. Raym. 1376, 1542; Str. 399, 609; 8 Mod. 307; and it should either be written by the drawer, or some person properly by him authorised. If drawn or signed by an agent, it is usual for him to sign as follows, " A B for
C D,"

C D," and if he does not express for whom he signs, he will be personally liable. If signed by one person for himself and partner, it is customary to sign " A B for A B and Company," or to that effect.

SIGNATURE, *what will be evidence of it.* A confession of signature is sufficient evidence against the party making it, but not against any other party. Cooper *v.* Le Blanc, Str. 1051; Hemmings *v.* Robinson, 1 Barnes 317.

SIGNATURE. In an action against several drawers, indorsers, or acceptors, an admission upon the pleadings by *one of his signature* will not exempt the plaintiff from proving it against the others if they contest it. Gray *v.* Palmer, Espinasse 125.

SIGNATURE of a partner or servant importing to have been made on the partnership or master's account, is to be considered as the signature of the partnership or master. Pinkney *v.* Hall, Ld. Raym. 175; Smith *v.* Jarvis, Ld. Raym. 1484; Carvick *v.* Vickery, Doug. 630.

SMALL NOTES and BILLS, see Appendix.

STAMPS. The law relative to stamps upon negotiable instruments rests upon the 31 G. 3.

R   c. 25.

c. 25. The duties are payable by the drawer
of the instrument, who, as well as the person
paying the same without its having been previously stamped, is subject to a penalty of 20*l.*
under the 10th section of the act. By the 19th
section also, unless the paper on which the instruments are written be stamped previously to
their being made, they shall not be received in
evidence in any Court whatsoever. If the bill
be unstamped, or bear an inferior stamp to that
prescribed by the act, the holder will have no
remedy, and the instrument will be invalid.
By 37 G. 3. c. 136. § 5, any bill made after
37 G. 3. c. 90, which shall be stamped with
a stamp of a different denomination to that required by the act, may, if the stamp be of
equal or *superior* value to the stamp required,
be stamped with the proper stamp on payment
of the proper duty, and forty shillings if the
bill is not due, or 10*l.* if it be due, and the
commissioners are thereupon to give a receipt
for the duty and penalty so paid on the back of
the bill, and such bill will be valid in any Court.
Previous to the passing of the above act a bill
stamped with an improper stamp was valid,
provided it was a stamp required under the
31st

31st G. 3. c. 25, and was of the same or greater value than the proper one, 31 G. 3. c. 25. § 19; but in the case of Manning *v.* Livie, Sit. after M. T. 1796 cor. Lord Kenyon, in an action on a note by an indorsee, the stamp appeared to be a seven-shilling deed stamp, and therefore his Lordship said could not be received.—The plaintiff was consequently non-suited.

STAMPS *on foreign bills.* Every bill drawn abroad must be stamped according to the laws of the country where it was made, otherwise the holder cannot recover upon it. Alves *v.* Hodgson, 7 T. R. 241; Esp. Ca. N. P. 528. See Appendix *Stamp Table.*

STAYING PROCEEDINGS. If the defendant in an action brought by the holder of a negotiable instrument is advised to settle the action in the first instance without further expence, he may take out a summons, or move the Court for a rule, calling on the plaintiff to shew cause, why on payment of the debt and costs, all further proceedings should not be stayed. If the holder of a bill of exchange bring separate actions against the acceptor, the drawer, and indorsers at the same time, the

Court

Court will stay the proceedings in any stage of the action against the drawer, or any one of the indorsers, upon payment of the amount of the bill and the costs of that particular action; but the action against the acceptor will only be stayed on the terms of his paying the costs in all the actions, he being the original defaulter. Chitty 193; 4 T. R. 691; Str. 515.

STYLE, see *Computation of Time.*

STOLEN BILL, see *Loss.*

SUPRA PROTEST, see *Acceptance supra Protest.*

T

TENDER. Bank notes are not a legal tender if specially objected to on that account at the time of the offer. 3 T. R. 554; 6 T. R. 335; though after such tender a creditor cannot arrest his debtor so as to hold him to bail. For by 38 G. 3. c. 1. § 8, no person shall be held to bail unless the affidavit of the debt allege that no offer has been made to pay the debt in Bank notes *payable on demand.*

TIME *for payment in a negotiable instrument,* see *Payment, Notice, Protest.*

TIME *allowed for acceptance.* It is customary to leave a bill presented for acceptance twenty-four hours, by way of giving the drawee an opportunity to look into his accounts with the

R 2   drawer,

drawer, and see whether he has effects or not. It is usual (although not demandable of right) for the payee or holder to leave the bill with him twenty-four hours after presentment, unless he accept in the interim, or declare his resolution not to accept. Ld. Raym. 281; Mar. 62; Beawes' Pl. 17. But it has been said that even this must not be done if the post goes out in the interim. Mar. 62; Com. Dig. tit. Merchant, F. 6. See *Acceptance*, p. 11.

TRANSFER *of bills, notes, or checks.* The transferable quality of written negotiable instruments is that which principally distinguishes them from almost every other security; and in consequence of the utility of these instruments in commercial transactions, they have been peculiarly favoured in Courts of Justice, and notwithstanding doubts formerly entertained relative to this point, it is decided that in bills, &c. payable to *order* or *bearer*, the transfer vests a right in the assignee to bring an action upon such assigned instrument in his own name. In general, however, unless there are some words giving authority to the holder to assign, he will have no right of action against any of the parties to the instrument but the assigner. 1 Salk. 133. Any words,

words, however, or facts proving the intention of the proprietor to make the instrument nego- tiable, will communicate a transferable quality to the instrument against such person. *

TRANSFER, *who may make it.* The right of transfer is in the payee, or in such person to whom such right has been by him transferred.

TRANSFER *when to be made.* Assignments of bills or notes are usually made after accep- tance and before payment; in some cases, however, a bill may be transferred after the time limited for its payment, in which case it has been held that such indorsement is equiva- lent to drawing a bill at sight. 1 T. R. 430; 1 Show. 164.

TRANSFER *of bills or notes after due,* see *Fraud, Over-due Bills.*

TRANSFER *of bills, &c. after due.* A trans- fer after payment cannot subject any of the parties to the instrument to any new engage- ments. 1 H. B. 89; Bull. N. P. 271. Bills or notes, however, if paid *in part* may be trans- ferred for the residue. Ld. Raym. 366; Carth. 466; 12 Mod. 213; 1 Salk. 65; 2 Wils. 262.

TRANSFER *of bills drawn in sets.* Each part must

* [All bills or notes which are drawn payable to bearer are transferred by the mere act of delivery. 1 Burr. 452. 3 Burr. 1516. 1 Bl. Rep. 485.]

must be delivered to the person in whose favour the transfer is made. See *Indorsement, Small Notes, Promissory Notes.*

TRANSFER *by delivery to a fictitious payee.* A transfer by delivery of a bill payable to a fictitious payee is valid against all the parties to it acquainted with that fact. 1 H. B. 600.

TRUSTEE. If a bill be made payable to A for the use of B, A is in this case trustee for B, who has the equitable interest, although the right of transfer in this case is in A.

U

USANCE is the time of *one*, *two*, or *three* months after the date of the bill, according to the custom of the places between which the exchanges run. Double or treble usance is double or treble the usual time, and half usance is half the time. Where it is necessary to divide a month upon an half usance, which is the case when the usance is either one month or three, the division, notwithstanding the difference in the length of the month, contains fifteen days. Mar. 93. The usances are calculated exclusive of the date of the bill. Bills drawn at usance are allowed the usual days of grace, and on the last of the three days the bill should be presented for payment.*

USURY

* [Where there is no date, and the payment is directed to be made so many days after date, the date is taken to be the day on which it was issued. Kyd 7. When a bill is payable at usance, it must be averred in pleading what that usance is; because usances differing according to the places between which they are reckoned, the court cannot, in any instance, take notice *ex officio* what they are. And that averment ascertaining the time when the bill is payable, it seems immaterial from what place the bill is stated to be dated. Buckley *v.* Campbell, 1 Salk. 13.]

USURY will vitiate negotiable instruments in the hands of an innocent holder. Bankers in discounting bills may retain five per cent. the customary commission, and reasonable incidental expences, over and above the interest or discount, without being guilty of usury. 3 Wils. 262; Moor 644; 1 Buls. 20; Winch qui tam *v.* Fenn, cited 2 T. R. 52.

V

VALUE RECEIVED. These words although usually inserted, are nevertheless not essential to the validity of negotiable instruments unless in particular cases, for value received is as much implied upon the face of every negotiable instrument as if these words had been actually expressed. Chitty 50. By 9 & 10 W. 3. c. 17, and 3 & 4 Anne, c. 9. § 4, the holder cannot recover interest and damages against the drawer and indorser in default of acceptance or payment, unless the bill contain the words *value received;* on this account, therefore, it is at all times adviseable to insert these words. See *Protest.**

VARIANCE.

* [The point is now fully settled, says Kyd, that these words are not necessary. Vid. 2 Strange 1212; 3 Wils. 207; Barnard K. B 282; 8 Mod. 267; 1 Show. 5, 497; 2 Ld. Raym. 1556, 1481; Lutw 889. Fortesc. Rep. 282; 1 Mod. Ent. 310. In France they are absolutely necessary. Beawes 490. If value received was in the bill or note, there is no occasion to prove the payment of that value. 2 Ld. Raym. 1556.]

VARIANCE. If in an action upon a negotiable instrument the plaintiff in his declaration set forth the instrument different from what it really is, such variance will be fatal. Bristow *v.* Wright, Doug. 667; Cowp. 600; 3 T. R. 178, 335, 643; 4 T. R. 471, 611; 1 Pul. and Bos. Rep. C. B. 7. See *Declaration.*

VERBAL ACCEPTANCE, see *Acceptance Verbal.*

VERDICT. The amount of the damages given by a Jury in an action upon a negotiable instrument comprises the following particulars, viz. the *principal sum due, interest,* and *expences,* being those incurred by *noting* or *protesting, postage,* and in foreign bills the *re-exchange.* See the respective heads.

W

WAIVER *of an acceptance.* The waiver of an acceptance may be either expressed or implied. An agreement to consider an acceptance at an end, or a message to the acceptor upon an accommodation bill that the business was settled with the drawer and he need give himself no further trouble, are express waivers. Master *v.* Miller, 4 T. R. 350; Walpole *v.* Pulteney, cited Doug. 236, 237, 248, 249; Black *v.* Peele, cited Doug. *supra.*

WAIVER. The receipt of the known consideration of the instrument is an implied waiver. Mason *v.* Hunt, Doug. 284, 297.

S　　　　WAIVER,

WAIVER, *how far constituted by receiving part payment from the acceptor*. If the holder of a bill or note receive a part of the money from the drawer, and take a promise from him upon the back of the bill for payment of the residue at an enlarged time, it shall in such case be left to a Jury to say whether this be not a waiver of the acceptance; but it should be left to them with strong observations that it is. Bayl. 56. cites Ellis *v.* Galindo, B. R. M. 24 G. 3, cited Doug. 250, *note*. See *Payment*.

WAIVER. Neglect to call upon an acceptor, or indulgence to any of the other parties, though for ever so long a time, shall not be considered as a waiver. Dingwall *v.* Dunster, Doug. 235, 247.

WAIVER, see *Discharge, Satisfaction, &c.*

WITNESSES *to a bill, when deemed competent*. Whether the payee in an action at the suit of the indorsee of a bill against the acceptor is a witness competent to prove that the bill was *originally void*, is a question of some doubt. 7 T. R. vide Esp. 332; Peake 6, 52, 244, acc. Esp. 10, 85, 298; Peake 40; Trials *per pais* 502; 12 Mod. 345; Holt 297, *contra*. But it has been decided that in an action against the
maker

maker of a note the indorser is a good witness to prove it paid. Peake 6, 52. In an action against the drawer of a bill the acceptor may prove that he had no effects in his hands, Esp. 332; and the maker of a note was admitted by Lord Mansfield, in an action against the indorser, to prove that the date had been altered Levy *v.* Essex, Sit. Mid. post M. T. 1775. A person whose name is on the bill as an indorser cannot be a witness to prove a property in it in himself, and that it was indorsed to the plaintiff without consideration. Esp. 85. A person supposed to be the drawer of a bill cannot be called upon to prove that *he did not draw it* without a release. 12 Mod. 345; Holt 297; Trials *per pais* 502.

WITNESSES *to an indorsement,* see *Small Notes.*

WORDS *which will constitute an acceptance,* see *Acceptance.*

WORDS *of negotiability,* see *Negotiability.*

WRIT OF INQUIRY. After judgment by default no evidence can be admitted against the validity of the instrument, although founded upon an usurious consideration, the validity

validity of the instrument being admitted by the defendant in suffering the Judgment to go by default. A writ of inquiry, however, in actions upon negotiable instruments is seldom executed, the usual practice being a reference to the Master to compute principal, interest, and costs. See *Evidence, Judgment by Default*.

APPENDIX.

APPENDIX.

ABSTRACTS OF THE ACTS

RELATIVE TO

𝔑𝔢𝔤𝔬𝔱𝔦𝔞𝔟𝔩𝔢 𝔖𝔢𝔠𝔲𝔯𝔦𝔱𝔦𝔢𝔰.

PROMISSORY NOTES,
3 & 4 ANNE, c. 9. § 1.

THE preamble to this act recites, that it having been held that promissory notes were not assignable or indorsable over within the custom of merchants to any other person, and that such person to whom such notes were payable could not maintain an action by the custom of merchants against the person who first drew and signed the same.

" To the intent to encourage trade and commerce, which will be much advanced if such notes shall have the same effect as bills of exchange, and shall be negotiated in like manner, enacts that all notes in writing payable to

any

any particular person or his order, or unto bearer, shall be made payable to such party; and also every such note payable to any person or persons, body politic and corporate, his, her, or their order, *shall be assignable or indorsable over in the same manner as inland bills of exchange are or may be, according to the custom of merchants; and that the persons, &c. to whom such sum of money is or shall be by such note made payable, shall and may maintain an action for the same in such manner as they might have done upon any inland bill of exchange made or drawn acccording to the custom of merchants against the persons, &c. who signed the same;* and any person or persons, &c. to whom such note is indorsed or assigned or the money therein mentioned ordered to be paid by indorsement thereon, shall and may maintain an action for such sum of money, against any of the parties, *in like manner as in cases of inland bills of exchange."*

PROTEST UPON INLAND BILLS,
9 & 10 W. 3. c. 17. § 1.

Bills of exchange, dated at or from any trading city or town, or any other place in England, Wales, or Berwick upon Tweed, of the sum of *five pounds* sterling, or upwards, (in which said bill or bills shall be acknowledged and expressed the said value to be received,) drawn payable at a certain number of days, weeks, or months from the date thereof, from and after presentation and acceptance of the said bill or bills of exchange (which acceptance shall be by the underwriting the same under the party's hand so accepting), and after the expiration of three days after the said bill or bills shall become due, the parties to whom the said bill or bills are made payable, his servant, agent, or assigns, may and shall cause the

the said bill or bills to be protested by a Notary Public;
and in default of such Notary Public, by any other substantial person of the city, town, or place, in the presence
of two or more credible witnesses, refusal or neglect being
first made of due payment of the same, which protest
shall be made and written under a fair written copy
of the said bill of exchange in the words or form following :—

" Know all men that I *A. B.* on the   day of
          at the usual place of abode of the said
have demanded payment of the bill of the which the
above is the copy, which the said   did not pay,
wherefore I the said *A. B.* do hereby protest the said
bill.

Dated this   day of   ."

BILLS LOST OR MISLAID,
9 & 10 W. 3. c. 17. § 3.

If any inland bill be lost or miscarry within the time
limited for its payment, the drawer shall, on security given
upon request to indemnify him if such bill be found again,
give another bill of the same tenor with the first.

The equity of this statute appears to comprehend indorsements also, and that the 3d and 4th Anne, c. 9.
which gives like remedies upon notes as were then in
use on inland bills, would extend it to notes.

PROTEST FOR NON-ACCEPTANCE IN WRITING.
9 W. 3. and 3 & 4 Anne, c. 9. § 4.

Upon presenting any inland bill of exchange, if the party
or parties on whom the same shall be drawn shall refuse
to accept the same under the party's hand so accepting,
                                                  the

the party to whom the said bill or bills are made payable, his servant, agent, or assigns, may and shall cause the said bill or bills to be protested for non-acceptance, as in case of foreign bills of exchange; for which protest there shall be paid *two shillings*, and no more.

3 & 4 Anne, c. 9. § 6.

By this act it is provided that no such protest shall be necessary either for non-acceptance or non-payment of any inland bill of exchange, unless the value be expressed to be received, and unless such bill be drawn for the payment of *twenty pounds sterling or upwards;* and that the protest required by this act for non-acceptance shall be made by such persons as are appointed by the preceding act of 9 and 10 W. 3. c. 17. to protest inland bills of exchange for non-payment thereof.

BILLS OR NOTES FOR GAMING CONSIDERATIONS,

9 Anne, c. 14. § 1.

" All notes, bills, or other securities whatsoever, given, granted, drawn, entered into, or executed by any person or persons whatsoever, where the whole, or any part of the consideration of such conveyances or securities shall be for any money or other valuable thing whatsoever won by gaming, or playing at *cards, dice, tables, tennis, bowls,* or *other game or games whatsoever*, or by betting on the sides or hands of such as do game at any of the games aforesaid, or *for the reimbursing or repaying any money knowingly lent* or advanced for such betting or gaming as aforesaid, or lent or advanced at the time and place of such play, to any person or persons so gaming

as

as aforesaid, or that shall during such play so play or bet, shall be utterly void, frustrate, and of none effect, to all intents and purposes whatsover."

BILLS OR NOTES TO BE CONSIDERED AS PAYMENT,
3 & 4 Anne, c. 9. § 7.

" If any person doth accept any *such* bill of exchange for and in satisfaction of any former debt or sum of money formerly due unto him, *the same shall be accounted and esteemed a full and complete payment of such debt*, if such person accepting of any such bill for his debt, doth not take his due course to obtain payment thereof by endeavouring to get the same accepted and paid, and make his protest as aforesaid, either for non-acceptance or non-payment thereof."

BILLS, NOTES, &c. FOR SIGNING BANKRUPTS' CERTIFICATES,
5 Geo. 2. c. 30. § 11.

Every bill, note, contract, agreement, or other security whatsoever, to be made known or given by any bankrupt or by any other person unto or to the use of or in trust for any creditor or creditors, or for the security of the payment of any debt or sum of money due from such bankrupt at the time of his becoming bankrupt and such bankrupt's discharge, as a consideration, or to the intent to persuade him, her, or them to consent to or sign any such allowance or certificate, shall be wholly void, and of no effect, and the monies thereby secured, or agreed to be paid, shall not be recovered or recoverable.

STAMPS.

ABSTRACTS OF ACTS

RELATIVE TO

Stamps for Bills, Notes, etc.

31 G. 3. c. 25.

THIS act imposes a stamp duty on the paper, &c. on which *any* bill of exchange shall be written; but from the conclusion of the section it is directed that the duty shall be paid by the person making such bills. From the 10th section, imposing a penalty upon any person writing or signing a bill on unstamped paper; and from the 19th section, which provides that the paper, &c. shall be stamped before writing the bill, and prohibits the stamping it afterwards, it is sufficiently obvious that the Legislature did not intend to extend it to bills drawn abroad.

Sections 2 and 3 relate to the duties payable upon negotiable instruments; for which see *Table of Stamps*.

Section

Section 4. " All notes and bills whatever which shall be issued by or on account of the Governor and Company of the Bank of England shall be freed and exempted from the stamp duties imposed by this act upon payment of 12,000*l.* annually into the Exchequer.

Section 5. Nothing in this act to charge any draught or order for the payment of money to the *bearer on demand*, bearing date on or before the day on which the same shall be issued, and at the place from which the same shall be drawn and issued, and drawn upon any banker or bankers, or person or persons acting as a banker or bankers, and residing and transacting the business of a banker or bankers, within ten miles of the place where such draught or order shall be actually drawn and issued.

Sections 7 and 8 regulate the duties payable upon notes re-issuable; for which see *Table.*

Section 10. " Any person writing or signing, or causing to be written or signed, or who shall accept or pay, or cause to be accepted or paid, any bill, note, draught, or order, liable to any duties imposed by this act, without the same being first duly stamped in the manner therein prescribed, *or upon which there shall not be some stamp or mark* resembling the same, shall for every such offence forfeit and pay the sum of *Ten Pounds.*"

Section 19. All vellum, parchment, and paper liable to any stamp duty in this act shall be stamped before any thing shall be engrossed, printed, or written thereupon ; and no bill of exchange, promissory note, or other note or order liable to the duties imposed by this act, or any of them, shall be pleaded or given in evidence in any Court, or admitted in any Court to be good, useful,

or

or available in law or equity, unless the vellum, parchment, or paper on which such bill of exchange, promissory note, or other note, draught, or order, receipt, discharge, acquittance, note, memorandum, or writing shall be engrossed, printed, written, or made, shall be stamped or marked with a lawful stamp or mark to denote the rate or duty, as by that act is directed, *or some higher rate or duty in that act contained.*

For the stamp duties imposed by the 2d, 3d, 7th, and 8th sections of this act upon inland bills, foreign bills, notes re-issuable, &c. see *Table of Stamps.*

SMALL NOTES,

15 G. 3. c. 51. § 1. *made perpetual by* 27 G. 3. c. 16.

All promissory or other notes, bills of exchange, or draughts, or undertakings in writing, being negotiable or transferable for the payment of any sum of money less than *twenty shillings* in the whole, are declared void and of no effect.

17 G. 3. c. 30. § 1.

After reciting the salutary consequences of the preceding act (15 G. 3.) and that if the provisions therein contained were extended to a further sum (but yet without prejudice to the convenience arising to the public from the negotiation of promissory notes and inland bills of exchange for the remittance of money in discharge of any balance of account or other debt), enacts, that all promissory notes, bills of exchange, or draughts, or undertakings in writing, negotiable or transferable for the payment of twenty shillings, or any sum of money above that sum and *less than five pounds*, &c. shall specify *the*

names

names and *places of abode* of the persons respectively to whom or to whose order the same shall be made payable, *and shall bear date before or at the time of drawing or issuing thereof,* and not on any day subsequent thereto, *and shall be made payable* within the space of *twenty-one days next after the day of the date thereof,* and shall not be transferable or negotiable after, the time thereby limited for payment thereof, and *every indorsement to be made thereon shall be made before the expiration of that time, and bear date at or not before the time of making thereof, and shall specify the name and place of abode of the person or persons to whom or to whose order the money contained in every such note, bill, draft, or undertaking is to be paid, and that the signing of every such note, bill, draft, or undertaking, and also of every such indorsement, shall be attested by one subscribing witness at the least,* and which said notes, bills of exchange, or draughts, or undertakings in writing, must be made or drawn in words to the purport or effect as set out in the schedules hereunto annexed, No. 1 and 2.

Schedule No. I.

(*Place*) (*Day*) (*Month*) (*Year*)

Twenty-one days after date I promise to pay to A. B. of (*Place*), or his order, the sum of

for value received by　　　　　　　C. D.

And the indorsement toties quoties.

(*Day*) (*Month*) (*Year*)

Pay the contents to G. H. of (*Place*), or his order.

Witness I. K.　　　　　　　　　　A. B.

　　　　　　　T　　　　　　　　No. II.

No. II.

(*Place*) (*Day*) (*Month*) (*Year*)

Twenty-one days after date pay to A. B. of (*Place*), or his order, the Sum of   value received, as advised by   C. D.

    To E. F. of (*Place*)

And the indorsement toties quoties.

          (*Day*) (*Month*) (*Year*)

Pay the contents to I. H. of (*Place*), or his order.

Witness L. M.   A. B.

Notes, indorsements, &c. contrary to this act shall be void, except notes of the Governor and Company of the Bank of England; for by the acts of 37 G. 3. c. 28. and 32 & 41 G. 3. all notes payable to bearer which have been issued by the Governor and Company of the Bank of England since the 2d day of March 1797, or which hereafter shall be issued by them, are made good and valid in law, notwithstanding their being made and issued for the payment of *less than five pounds;* and the acts of the 15th and 17th G. 3. so far as they relate either to the making void of promissory notes, or draughts, or undertakings in writing payable on demand to the bearer thereof, for any sum of money *less than five pounds* in the whole, or to restrain the publishing, or uttering, or negotiating of any such notes, draughts, or undertakings, are suspended.

SELECT CASES

BILLS, NOTES, AND CHECKS,

RELATIVE TO

Acceptance, Bankruptcy, Costs, Notice, Present-ment, Protest, Re-exchange, &c.

———————

ACCEPTANCE ABSOLUTE, *what will amount to one.*

Pillans and another v. *Van Mierop,* Burr. 1663. White drew on the plaintiffs at Rotterdam for 800*l.*, and pro-posed to give them credit upon the defendant's house in London; the plaintiffs paid White's bill, and wrote to the defendants to know " whether they would accept such bills as they (the plaintiffs) should draw in about a month upon them for 800*l.* on White's credit." The defendants answered, that they would; but White having failed before the month elapsed, the defendants wrote to the plaintiffs not to draw. The plaintiffs did however draw, and on the defendant's refusal to pay the bills brought this action. The Jury found a verdict for the defendants; but upon an application for a new trial, as upon a verdict against evidence,

dence, and two arguments upon it, the Court was unanimous that the defendant's letter was a virtual acceptance of such bills as the plaintiff should draw to the amount of 800*l*., and the rule was made absolute.

Powell v. *Monnier*, 1 Atk. 611. A bill was sent by the post to the drawee for acceptance; he entered it in his bill book (which was his practice with all bills he received, whether he meant to accept them or not), wrote upon it the number of the entry, and kept it ten days; on the tenth he wrote upon it the day of the month, and returned it, saying he could not accept it: and per Lord Hardwicke, " it has been said to be the custom of merchants, that if a man underwrites any thing, be it what it may, it amounts to an acceptance; but if there were nothing more than this in the case, I should think it of little avail to charge the defendant;" but he decided that a letter the drawee had written amounted to an acceptance.

Moor v. *Whitby*, B. R. Tr. 10 G. 3. Bull. N. P. 270. A bill drawn by Newton on Whitby was presented for acceptance, and Whitby wrote upon it, " Mr. Jackson, please to pay this note, and place it to Mr. Newton's account, R. Whitby;" it was insisted that this was no acceptance, but merely a direction to Jackson to pay it out of a particular fund, and if there was no fund, there was to be no payment; sed per Cur. this is a direction to Jackson to pay the money; and it signifies not to what account it is to be placed; that is between Jackson and Whitby only; this is clearly an acceptance.

Powell v. *Jones*, Espinasse 17. In an action against the defendant as acceptor of a bill, the only evidence to prove the acceptance, was, that when the bill was called for he returned it, and said, " there is your bill, it is all right."

Lord

Lord Kenyon thought these words could by no implication amount to an acceptance, and nonsuited the plaintiff.

Acceptance Conditional.

Cox v. *Coleman*, M. 6 G. 2. cited arguendo Ann. 75. A foreign bill drawn on defendant was protested for nonacceptance and returned, and afterwards defendant told the plaintiff, " if the bill comes back, I will pay it;" and this was held a good acceptance.

Julian v. *Shobrooke*, 2 Wils. 9. The defendant accepted a bill to pay, *when in cash, for the cargo of the ship Thetis;* and on being sued, moved in arrest of judgment that a conditional acceptance was not good; but the court held otherwise, and over-ruled the objection.

Pierson v. *Dunlop*, Cowp. 571. An answer that the bill would not be accepted till a navy bill was paid, was held a conditional acceptance to pay when the navy bill should be discharged.

Acceptance Partial.

Wegersloffe v. *Keene*, Str. 214. A foreign bill for the sum of 127*l*. 18*s*. 4*d*. was drawn on the defendant, and he accepted it to pay 100*l*. part thereof; he was sued upon this acceptance, and on demurrer to the replication, insisted that a partial acceptance was not good within the custom of merchants; but the Court held otherwise, and judgment was given for the plaintiff.

Petit v. *Benson*, Comb. 452. A bill was accepted to be paid, half in money and half in bills, and the question was, whether there could be a qualification of an acceptance, and it was proved by divers merchants that there might, for he that might refuse the bill totally might accept it in part; but that the holder was not bound to acquiesce in such acceptance.

T 2   ACCEPTANCE

Acceptance Verbal.

In Pillans *v*. Van Mierop, Lord Mansfield said, a verbal acceptance was binding; and in Sproat *v*. Matthews, 1 Term Rep. 182. it was taken for granted by the Court and Bar that a verbal acceptance was good.

Acceptance *waiver of*.

Walpole v. *Pulteney*, cited Dougl. 236, 237—248, 249. Walpole held a bill accepted by Pulteney, but agreed to consider his acceptance as at an end, and wrote in his bill book, opposite the entry of this bill, " Mr. Pulteney's acceptance at an end." Walpole kept the bill from 1772 to 1775, without calling upon Pulteney, and then brought this action. The Jury found a verdict for the plaintiff; but the Court of Exchequer thought the verdict wrong, and granted a new trial, upon which the Jury found for the defendant.

Black v. *Peele*, cited Dougl. 236, 237—248, 249. Black arrested Peele as acceptor of a bill drawn by Dallas, but on finding that the acceptance was an accommodation one, his attorney took a security from Dallas, and sent word to Peele that he had settled with Dallas, and that Peele need give himself no further trouble; Dallas afterwards became bankrupt, upon which Black again sued Peele; but it was held that as Black had in express words discharged Peele, the action could not be maintained.

Mason v. *Hunt*, Dougl. 284, 297. Rowland Hunt agreed that his partner Thomas Hunt should, on consignment of a cargo and an order for its insurance, accept bills for 3600*l*. The cargo was consigned, the order for insurance given, and Thomas Hunt effected the insurance, but he refused to accept the bills; after some negotiation, the plaintiff being the holder, signed a memorandum, by which,

which, after stating that the consignment had been made on account of the bills, and that the Hunts being apprehensive that the net proceeds might not be sufficient to discharge them, had refused to accept, he accepted the bill of lading and policy, and undertook to apply the net proceeds, when in cash, as far as they would go to the credit of the payee, in part payment of the bills ; the plaintiff afterwards sued the Hunts, and insisted that Rowland Hunt's agreement was an acceptance ; but after a verdict for the defendant, and time taken to consider, upon a rule to shew cause why there should not be a new trial, the whole Court was clear that by the memorandum the plaintiff had waived all right to insist on Rowland Hunt's agreement, for it was obvious that the whole consideration of the acceptance was the consignment, upon which there would be a commission and the policy, and these the plaintiff had taken to himself.

Ellis v. *Galindo*, B.R. M. 24 G. 3. cited Dougl. 250, note. James Galindo drew upon his brother for 30*l*. in favour of the plaintiff; when the bill became due James paid the plaintiff 3*l*. 15*s*. 4*d*. and indorsed a promise to pay the remainder in three months. Three years elapsed, and then the plaintiff sued the drawee upon his acceptance. Lord Mansfield thought the defendant discharged, and nonsuited the plaintiff. An application was made for a new trial, when Lord Mansfield said, he thought the case did not interfere with that of Dingwall v. Dunster, but a rule to shew cause was granted: after cause was shewn, Lord Mansfield said, " the doubt is, whether the question should not have been left to the Jury, it being a question of intention arising out of the circumstances." Judge Willes thought it should have been left to the Jury; and per Judge Buller,

Buller, " I rather think the case should have gone to the Jury, but am not therefore of opinion that there ought to be a new trial; the indorsement could not have been meant as an additional security, for the drawer was equally liable before. I should have left the question to the Jury, but with very strong observations, and as the demand is so small, I do not think there ought to be a new trial." Rule discharged.

Dingwall v. *Dunster*, Dougl. 235, 247. Dunster lent Wheate his acceptance, which became due the 13th of December 1774; it was then in the hands of Dingwall, but he finding that Wheate was the real debtor wrote to his Attorney in February and November 1775 for payment, received interest upon the bill from Wheate, and suffered several years to elapse without calling on Dunster; on the 13th of February 1775, Dunster wrote to thank Dingwall for not proceeding against him, and said he had been informed by a person Dingwall had sent that Wheate had taken up the bill; but Dingwall took no notice of this letter; he afterwards sued Dunster, for whom the Jury found; but upon a rule to shew cause why there should not be a new trial, the whole court held that there was nothing in the plaintiff's conduct to discharge Dunster; that it meant nothing more than an indulgence to him, and that he would try to recover from the drawer if he could; but by Lord Mansfield, no use has been made of the defendant's letter; probably the fact did not warrant him in asserting that a person the plaintiff sent had told him that Wheate had taken up the bill; had the plaintiff by any thing in his conduct confirmed him in such a belief, it might have altered the case.

BANK-

BANKRUPTCY *of Parties to Bills or Notes.*

Ex parte *Wildman*, 1 Atk. 109. 2 Vez. 113. Wildman held bills drawn by Buckle and accepted by Vanhylik; Vanhylik failed, and made a composition with his creditors, and Buckle became bankrupt. Wildman having received nothing under Vanhylik's composition, proved his whole debt under Buckle's commission, but before any dividend was made, he received 2s. 6d. in the pound out of Vanhylik's estate. Buckle's assignees then contended that he ought to deduct the 2s. 6d. in the pound out of his proof, and take a dividend upon the balance only ; but Lord Hardwicke held that as the whole sum was due when he proved his debt, and the dividend and composition would not amount to 20s. in the pound upon his debt, he was entitled to a dividend upon his whole debt ; and per Lord Hardwicke, " In cases of bills or notes, where there is a drawer, and perhaps several indorsers, suppose two of these persons become bankrupts, the holder may prove his *whole debt* under each commission, and is entitled to receive satisfaction out of both estates, according to the dividends to be made, until he has received satisfaction for his whole debt ; for he has a double security, and it is neither law nor equity to take it from him ; but if before the bankruptcy of one he had received payment of part from the other, he could only have proved the residue under the latter bankruptcy, as the form of proving his debt shews, because no more would remain due to him." To the same effect are the cases of ex parte Royd and ex parte Bennett, cited 2 Vez. 114. And see Cooke's Bankrupt Laws, 170.

Cooper v. *Pepys*, 1 Atk. 106. The holders of notes drawn by Reeves, and payable to Andree, accepted 6s. in the

pound

pound from Andree, and Reeves having become bankrupt, the question was, Whether they might prove the
whole debt under his commission? and Lord Hardwicke
held they could not, but that the 6s. in the pound must
go in discharge of so much of the debt, and they could
only prove the remaining 14s. The same point was ruled
in ex parte Ryswick, 2 P. Williams 89, ex parte Lefebvre,
2 P. Williams 409. See Cooke's Bankrupt Laws, 170.

CONSIDERATIONS ILLEGAL.

Robinson v. *Bland*, Burr. 1077. A bill of exchange was
partly for money lent at the time and place of play, and
partly for money lost at play; and on a case reserved the
Court held that the plaintiff could recover nothing upon
the bill, but that he might recover the money lent on a
count for money lent.

Bowyer v. *Bampton*, Str. 1155. Several notes given by
Bampton to Church for money lent to game with, were
indorsed by Church to the plaintiff for a full and valuable consideration, and the plaintiff had no knowledge that
any part of the consideration from Church to Bampton
was for money lent for gaming; and after two arguments
upon the case reserved the Court held that the plaintiff
could not maintain the action, for it would be making the
notes of use to the lender if he could pay his debts with
them, and it would tend to evade the act, on account of
the difficulty of proving notice on an indorsee; and the
plaintiff would not be without remedy, for he might sue
Church on his indorsement.

Lowe v. *Waller*, Dougl. 708—736. The defendant was
acceptor of a bill, which he gave to Harris and Stratton
upon an usurious contract; Harris and Stratton indorsed
it

it to the plaintiff for a valuable consideration, and the plaintiff had no notice of the usury ; upon a case reserved the question was, Whether the usury between Harris and Stratton and the defendant was a defence against an indorsee who took the bill bona fide, and paid a valuable consideration for it? and after time taken to consider, the Court held it was; and though Lord Mansfield had a wish the law should turn out in favour of the plaintiff, the Court found the words of the act too strong, and could not get over the case of Bowyer *v.* Bampton, Str. 1155.

Daniel v. *Cartony*, Espinasse 274. Scott drew a bill on the defendant payable to his own order, and discounted it with Greensill, who took 18*l.* per cent. discount; it was afterwards indorsed to the plaintiff, and defendant could not impeach *that* transaction; and per Lord Kenyon, " This is no defence ; had the note been originally given on an usurious transaction, or for an usurious consideration, it would have been void in the hands of even a bona fide holder; but usury in any intermediate transaction respecting it can never make it void in the hands of a bona fide indorsee, where there was no usury in the original transaction.

COSTS.

Golding v. *Grace*, Blackst. 749. The indorser of a bill obtained a rule nisi to stay proceedings on payment of the debt and the costs of the writ; the plaintiff insisted that he was entitled to be paid for drawing declarations against the defendant and the drawer; and it was agreed, that if any was to be paid for, the plaintiff was entitled to be paid for both ; but the Court held that the application to

pay

pay debt and costs was made so early that the plaintiff was only entitled to the costs of the writ.

Windham v. *Withers*, Str. 515. The plaintiff having obtained judgments against the drawer and indorser of a note, the principal in one, and the costs in both were offered him, which he refused; and the Court granted a rule to restrain him from taking out execution, and intimated that they would have punished him, had he taken out execution upon both judgments.

Smith v. *Woodcock*—*Same* v. *Dudley*, 4 Term Rep. 691. The holder of a bill brought actions against the acceptor, the drawer, and two indorsers; the drawer and one of the indorsers obtained a rule nisi to stay proceedings against them on payment of the bill and the costs of the actions against *them;* the plaintiff insisted that the costs of the other actions should be also paid: sed per Cur. " That is only necessary where the application comes from the acceptor, who is the original defaulter, and against whom all the costs occasioned by his default may be recovered." Rule absolute.

Costs *proveable under Bankruptcy.*

Anon. 1 Atk. 140. The question was, Whether the costs and charges incurred by protesting bills after a commission of bankruptcy issued could be proved? and Lord Hardwicke ordered that the costs of the protests arising before the commission, should be proved, but no part of the costs arising afterwards.

Ex parte *Moore*, 2 Bro. Cha. Ca. 597. Previous to the 5th of May 1785, Mrs. Tyler accepted several bills drawn upon her by Moore, and on that day committed an act of bankruptcy, but no commission issued until the 9th

of

of March 1786; the bills became due between May 1785 and March 1786, and Mrs. Tyler not paying them, Moore did; he also paid 298*l.* for damages and charges, and the interest amounted to 46*l.* 10*s.* The commissioners allowed Moore to prove the sums for which the bills were drawn, but would not let him prove the interest or the sum paid for damages and charges, upon which he petitioned the Chancellor; but the Chancellor held that as the time when the act of bankruptcy was committed was ascertained, he could not carry the damages beyond that time; and the petition was disallowed.   .

DAYS OF GRACE.

Coleman v. *Sayer*, 1 Barnard, B. R. In an action upon an inland bill payable six days after sight, one question was, Whether three days grace are allowed where a bill is payable at certain days after sight, as well as where it is payable upon sight? and Chief Justice Raymond said they were allowable in one case as well as in the other. Another question was, Whether they were allowable upon inland as well as upon foreign bills? and the Common Sergeant and Foreman of the Jury said it was the constant practice in the city to allow them in both cases, upon which Chief Justice Raymond said he would not alter it; but the plaintiff was non-suited on another point.

LOST BILLS, NOTES, &c.

Anon. Ld. Raym. 738. Salk. 126. 3 Salk. 71. B lost a bank bill payable to A or bearer; C found it, and assigned it for a valuable consideration to D, who got a new bill for it from the Bank. Trover was then brought

U   against

against D for the first bill, but by Chief Justice Holt, " the action will not lie against *him*, because he took it for a valuable consideration, though it would against C, as he had no title; but payment to C would have indemnified the Bank."

Miller v. *Race*, Burr. 452. A Bank note payable to Wm. Finney or bearer was stolen out of the mail in the night of the 11th of December 1756, and on the 12th came to the hands of the plaintiff for a full and valuable consideration, in the usual course of his business, and without any knowledge that it had been taken out of the mail; he afterwards presented it at the Bank for payment, and the defendant being one of the clerks stopped it, upon which an action of trover was brought; and upon a case reserved upon the point whether the plaintiff had a sufficient property in the note to entitle him to recover, the Court was clear in opinion that he had, and that the action was well brought.

Grant v. *Vaughan*, Burr. 1516. Vaughan gave Bicknell a draught upon his banker, payable to " Ship Fortune or Bearer." Bicknell lost it, and the plaintiff afterwards took it bona fide, in the course of trade, and paid a valuable consideration for it. The banker refused to pay it, upon which the plaintiff brought this action against Vaughan. Lord Mansfield left it to the Jury to consider first, whether the plaintiff came to the possession of the bill fairly and bona fide; and secondly, whether such draught was in fact and practice negotiable; and the Jury found for the defendant. But upon an application for a new trial, and cause shewn against it, the Court was clear that the second point ought not to have been left to the Jury, because it was clear that such draughts were negotiable,

tiable, and if the Jury thought the plaintiff took the note
fairly and bona fide, of which there appeared to be no
doubt, he was entitled to recover. A new trial was accordingly granted, in which the plaintiff recovered the
money.

NOTICE.

In *Russel* v. *Langstaffe*, Dougl. 497, 515. Lee said arguendo, it had frequently been ruled by Lord Mansfield
at Guildhall, that it is not an excuse for not making a
demand on a note or bill, or for not giving notice of non-
payment, that the drawer or acceptor has become a bankrupt, as many means may remain of obtaining payment
by the assistance of friends, or otherwise, and Lord Mansfield, who was in Court, did not deny the assertion; this
dictum was also referred to arguendo in Bickerdike *v.*
Bollman, 1 Term Rep. 408.

Blesard v. *Hurst and another*, Burr. 2670. The defendants indorsed a bill to the plaintiff, and he indorsed
it over; his indorsee presented it for acceptance a month
before it was due, and acceptance was refused; it was
afterwards presented for payment, and payment was refused, of which notice was given to the defendants, but
they had no notice of the refusal to accept. The drawer
was a bankrupt before the bill was due, but he continued
in credit three weeks after the presentment for acceptance.
Three days after the notice one of the defendants called
on the plaintiff at Bradford, on his way to Leeds, and said
he would take up the bill as he returned; but on his return he said he was advised he was not bound to do it,
upon which this action was brought; and on a case reserved the Court held, that though the holder might not
have

have been obliged to present the bill for acceptance, yet
as he did he ought to have given notice of the refusal,
and that by not doing so he had taken the risque upon
himself, and notwithstanding the promise of one of them
the defendants had judgment.

Tindal v. *Brown*, 1 T. R. 167. A note which became
due the 5th of October was presented at ten in the morning, and the maker not being at home, word was left for
him where it lay; the holder sent again on the 6th, when the
maker promised to take it up within the banking hours,
which were from 9 to 4; on the 7th the holder sent again
to the maker, and the note not being paid, gave notice to
the defendant, who was an indorser, but the defendant
said he had made it his own; the maker had told him on
the 6th that he could not pay it, and desired the defendant would; all the parties lived at Bristol; the Jury found
for the plaintiff, but upon a rule to shew cause why there
should not be a new trial, and cause shewn, the Court
granted a new trial; Lord Mansfield said, " What is reasonable notice is a question partly of fact, and partly of
law; it may depend in some measure on facts, such as the
distance at which the parties live, the course of the post,
&c. but wherever a rule can be laid down with respect to
this reasonableness, *that* should be decided by the Court,
and adhered to for the sake of certainty." Per Judge Willes
" New credit was given to the maker, and I cannot consider notice from the maker equal to notice from the
holder. Judge Ashhurst, " The reasonableness ought to
be settled as a question of law; the next day at the most
is as long as is necessary in a case like this; if the parties
live at a small distance, this is a sufficient time: if at a
greater, they should write by the next post. Notice means
                                        something

something more than knowledge, because it is competent to the holder to give credit to the maker. It is not enough to say that the maker does not intend to pay, but that the holder does not intend to give credit; the party ought to know whether the holder intends to give credit to the maker or to resort to him." Per Judge Buller, " *When* the post goes out is a matter of fact; when that is established, it is a matter of law what notice is reasonable; as to giving time, the holder does it at his peril, and that is enough to decide the case; the purpose of giving notice is to let the party know that he is looked to for payment, that he may have his remedy over by an early application; if it shews that the holder has given time, it discharges the party; it ought to purport that the holder looks to him for payment, and a notice from another person cannot be sufficient, it must come from the holder." Upon the second trial there was contradictory evidence whether the notice from the maker was on the 6th or the 7th, and the Jury found again for the plaintiff, but the Court said it was a verdict against law, and granted another new trial.

Saunderson v. *Judge.* The holder of a note wrote to the defendant, who was one of the indorsers, to say it was dishonoured, and put the letter in the post, but there was no evidence that it ever reached the defendant, and the Court held that sending the letter by the post was quite sufficient.

Gee v. *Brown*, St. 792. The holder of an inland bill gave the acceptor time by intervals from the 14th of May when the bill became due, to the 7th of June, and then sued the drawer, but there being no notice to him, Chief Justice Eyre held the loss ought to fall on the plaintiff.

Rogers v. *Stephens*, 2 Term Rep. 713. In an action against the drawer of a foreign bill an objection was taken that there was no protest, but it appearing that the defendant had no effects in the hands of the drawees when the bill was drawn or afterwards, and that on being pressed for payment by the plaintiff's agent after the bill was dishonoured he had said it must be paid; Lord Kenyon thought a protest or notice unnecessary, and directed the Jury to find for the plaintiff, which they did. A rule was afterwards granted to shew cause why there should not be a new trial, and it was stated *then*, and upon the shewing cause that the defendant had really been prejudiced by the want of notice to the amount of the bill, that he had advanced money to one Calvert to the amount before the bill was drawn, that Calvert desired him to draw on the drawees as Calvert's agents, that he did so on a supposition that Calvert had effects in their hands, that he afterwards settled with Calvert, and upon a reliance that the bill was paid, delivered him up effects to more than the value of the bill, and that Calvert was since insolvent; that the defendant was prepared with evidence to this effect, but that Lord Kenyon delivered it as his opinion that it did not make a protest or notice necessary. Lord Kenyon did not recollect that this evidence was offered, but he and all the Court thought it answered by the defendant's admission that the bill must be paid, because that was an admission that the plaintiff had a resort to him upon the bill, and that he had received no damage by the want of notice, and was a promise to pay. The rule was discharged.

Bickerdike and another, assignees of Reichard, v. *Bollman*, 1 Term Rep. 405. The only question upon a case reserved

reserved was, Whether a bill the bankrupt had drawn in
favour of the petitioning creditor, upon a man who then
and from that time till the bill became due, was one of
the bankrupt's creditors, had discharged so much of the
petitioning creditor's debt, no notice having been given
of its dishonour to the bankrupt? and the Court, after
argument, was of opinion it had not, because the reason
why notice is in general necessary is, that the drawer may
without delay withdraw his effects from the drawee, and
that no injury may happen to him from the want of notice; but where the drawer has no effects in the hands of
the drawee he cannot be injured, and is not entitled to
any notice.

Goodall v. *Dolley*. In this case upon the application for
a new trial, the plaintiff's counsel offered an affidavit that
the drawer had no effects in the hands of the drawee, but
the Court thought *that* made no difference, the action
being brought against the payee; but by Judge Buller,
" Had the action been against the drawer I should have
been willing to let in the affidavit; that would be like the
case of Bickerdike v. Bollman; if the drawer has no effects in the hands of the drawee he cannot be injured by
want of notice."

De Bert v. *Atkinson*, 2 H. Bl. 336. In an action against
the payee of a note it appeared that the note was not presented for payment till the day after it became due, and
that no notice was given to the defendant till five days
after such presentment; but it also appearing that the defendant gave no value for the note, that he lent his name
merely to give it credit, and that he knew at the time
the maker was insolvent, Chief Justice Eyre directed the
Jury to find for the plaintiff, which they did. A rule to
shew

shew cause why there should not be a new trial was
afterwards granted, and upon cause shewn, per Chief
Justice Eyre, " If the maker is not known to be insolvent, insolvency will not excuse the want of an early
demand; but knowledge excludes all presumption which
would otherwise arise; here the money was to be raised
upon the defendant's credit; he meant to guarantee the
payment, and no loss could happen to him from the want
of notice." And per Judge Buller, " The general rule is
only applicable to fair transactions, where the bill or note
has been given for value in the ordinary course of trade,
it is said insolvency does not take away the necessity of
notice; that is true, where value has been given, but no
further; here the defendant lent his name merely to give
credit to the note, and was not an indorser in the common course of business." Judges Heath and Rooke con-
curring, the rule was discharged.

Corney v. *Da Costa*, Espinasse 302. Da Costa and Co.
compounded with their creditors, and to secure the composition drew notes in favour of the defendant, which he
indorsed to the creditors. The defendant took effects of
Da Costa and Co. at the time, to the amount of the composition; and an action being brought against him upon
one of these indorsements, he insisted that he had no
notice of the non-payment of the note until five weeks
after it was due; but Judge Buller held he was not entitled to notice, and the plaintiff had a verdict.

Staples v. *Okines*, Espinasse, 332. In an action against
the drawer of a bill the defence was want of notice; the
plaintiff thereupon called the acceptor, who proved that
when the bill was drawn he was indebted to the defendant in more than the amount of the bill, but that he then
represented

represented to the defendant that it would not be in his power to provide for the bill when it should become due, and that it was therefore then understood between them that the defendant should provide for it; and it was contended that this superseded the necessity of giving the defendant notice: but Lord Kenyon held it did not, and nonsuited the plaintiff.

PRESENTMENT *for* ACCEPTANCE *or Payment.*

Muilman v. *D'Eguino*, 2 H. Bl. 565. In debt on bond conditioned to pay certain bills drawn on India at sixty days after sight in case they should be returned protested, defendant pleaded that they were not presented for acceptance within a reasonable time after the drawing; it appeared that they were drawn the 5th of March 1793, that they were indorsed on that day by defendant to plaintiffs, who procured them for a house at Paris; that plaintiffs sent immediate advice to the house at Paris, and on receiving their directions on the 30th of April sent them to India, where they arrived the 3d of October; on the 5th of October the holder wrote to the drawee, who was from home, desiring him to accept the bills, and on the 17th of October he sent an answer of refusal; some of the bills were thereupon protested on the 29th of October, and the rest the 18th of November. Chief Justice Eyre left the case to the Jury, but told them he thought the bills had been sent to India in time, as they were put up here for negotiation, and were therefore liable to be delayed, and that they were presented in India in time after their arrival. The Jury found for the plaintiff, and on a rule to shew cause why there should not be a new trial, and cause shewn, the Court

was

was satisfied with the verdict, and the plaintiff had judgment. Chief Justice Eyre said, " It is not necessary to
lay down any new rule as to bills of exchange payable at
sight, or within a given time afterwards; if it were, I
should feel great anxiety not to clog the negotiation of
bills circumstanced like these. It would be a very seri-
ous and difficult thing to say that a person paying a foreign bill, in the way these were bought, should be
obliged to transmit it by the first opportunity to the
place of its destination. There would also be a great difficulty in saying *at what time* such a bill should be presented for acceptance. The Courts have been very cautious in fixing any time for presenting for acceptance an
inland bill payable at a certain period after sight, and it
seems to me more necessary to be cautious with respect
to a foreign bill payable in that manner. I think, indeed, the holder is bound to present the bill in reasonable time, in order that the period may commence from
which the payment is to take place; but the question,
What is reasonable time? must depend on the particular
circumstances of the case; and it must always be for the
Jury to determine whether any laches are imputable to
the plaintiff." Per Judge Buller, " The only rule I know
of which can be applied to the case of bills of exchange is,
that due diligence must be used. Due diligence is the only
thing to be looked at, whether the bill be foreign or inland, and whether it be payable at sight, at so many days
after, or in any other manner. But I think a rule may
thus far be laid down as to laches with regard to bills
payable at sight, or a certain time after sight, namely,
that they ought to be put in circulation; and if a bill
drawn at three days sight were kept out in that way for
a year,

a year, I cannot say there would be laches; but if instead of putting it in circulation the holder were to lock it up for any length of time, I should say that he would be guilty of laches: but farther than this no rule can be laid down." Per Judge Heath, " No rule can be laid down as to the time for presenting bills payable at sight, or at a given time afterwards. In the French ordinances of 1673, in Postlethwaite and Marius, it is said, " That a bill payable at sight *or at will* is the same thing."

Appleton v. *Sweetapple*, B. R. M. 23 G. 3. A bill payable in London on demand was given to the plaintiff in London at one o'clock in the afternoon, and he did not present it till next morning; the question was, Whether he presented it in time? Lord Mansfield left the point to the Jury, who found for the defendant! but the Court granted a new trial because the question was a matter of law upon which the Judge should have decided; the Jury found again for the defendant, but against the Judge's direction; a second new trial was granted, and the Jury again found for the defendant; and then the Court refused to interfere.

Turner and others v. *Mead*, Str. 416. The defendants paid the Sword Blade Company (the plaintiffs) two banker's notes at three o'clock in the afternoon, and the next morning their servant left them at the banker's in order to call for the money in the evening, it then being the custom with the plaintiffs and the bank to send out their notes in the morning and to call for the money in the afternoon. The plaintiffs' servant called for the money between four and five in the afternoon, and the banker had just stopped payment; and because the plaintiffs had done nothing more than was usual in leaving the
notes

notes in the morning without taking the money, Chief Justice Pratt directed the Jury to find for them, which they did.

Hoar v. *Da Costa*, Str. 910. The defendant paid the plaintiff a banker's note at twelve, he put it into the Bank at one, and at ten the next morning the runner from the Bank carried it with other notes, and left them, as was then usual, to call again for the money: he called at eleven, and was told that the banker's servant was gone to the Bank; he called again at two, when the banker said he was going to stop, and refused payment, but he paid small notes till four o'clock. The defendant gave notice to the plaintiff the next morning: the question was, Whether this note was payment to the plaintiff? It was insisted for the defendant, that if the note had been tendered by itself it would have been paid; and for the plaintiff, that if there had been no demand there would have been no laches, being within a day after the receipt. Chief Justice Raymond said there was no standing rule, and left it to the Jury, who found for the plaintiff.

Manwaring v. *Harrison*, Str. 508. On Saturday the 17th of Septemper, about two o'clock, Harrison gave Manwaring a banker's note dated the fifth of September, and payable to Harrison or order on demand; Manwaring paid it away the same afternoon to J. S. and he presented it for payment on the Tuesday morning as soon as the shop was open; but the banker stopped payment at that time. Manwaring paid the money to J. S. and brought this action to recover it from Harrison. Chief Justice Pratt left it to the Jury whether there had been any neglect, and observed, that as Harrison had kept it

eleven

eleven days he probably would not have demanded payment sooner than J. S. did. The Jury wished to leave it
to the Court whether there had been a reasonable time;
but the Chief Justice told them *they* were the judges of
that; upon which they found for the defendant, and
gave it as their opinion, that a person who did not
demand a banker's note in two days, took the credit on
himself.

Collins v. *Butler*, Str. 1087. The maker of a note shut
up his house before the note became due, and in an action
against an indorser the question was, Whether the plaintiff had shewn sufficient in proving that the house was shut
up? and Chief Justice Lee thought not, but that he should
have given in evidence that he enquired after the maker,
or attempted to find him out.

Moor v. *Warren*, Str. 415. The defendant gave the
plaintiff a banker's note at two o'clock in the afternoon,
and he tendered it for payment the next morning at nine;
the banker stopped a quarter of an hour before; and
Chief Justice Pratt told the Jury the loss should fall on
the defendant, there being no laches in the plaintiff, who
had demanded the money as soon as was usual in the
course of dealing, and that keeping the note till next
morning could not be construed as giving a new credit to
the banker; and the Jury found for the plaintiff. In
Holmes v. *Barry*, Str. 415. the circumstances were the
same, and King, Chief Justice of the Common Pleas, gave
a similar direction, and the Jury found accordingly.

Fletcher v. *Sandys*, Str. 1248. A banker's note was paid
to the plaintiff after dinner, and he sent it for payment
the next morning; but the banker had stopped payment;
and Chief Justice Lee ruled that there were no laches in

the plaintiff, and that in all these cases there must be a reasonable time allowed, consistent with the nature of circulating paper credit.

East India Company v. *Chitty*, Str. 1175. At half past eleven in the morning of the 18th of January the defendant paid the East India Company's Cashier a banker's note, and they did not send it for payment till the next day at two, at which time the banker stopped payment. The question was, Who should bear the loss? and upon examining the merchants it was held that the Company had made it their own by not sending it out the afternoon they received it, or at furthest the next morning; and the Jury found accordingly for the defendant.

Nicholson v. *Gouthit*, 2 H. Bl. 609. Gouthit and Burton undertook to guarantee an instalment on the debts of Greens, and for that purpose Greens drew notes payable to Gouthit at Drury and Co.'s which Gouthit and Burton indorsed, after which they were delivered to the creditors. Before they became due Gouthit enquired at Drury and Co.'s if they had any effects, and on their saying they had not, he desired them to send the notes to him, and he would pay them; many notes were accordingly presented and paid, but the note in question not being presented till three days after it was due, Gouthit refused to pay it. Burton had supplied him with money to take up all the notes, but as this was not presented when due, he had returned the money destined to pay it. An action was brought against Gouthit, and upon the trial Chief Justice Eyre thought as he knew the note would not be paid at Drury and Co.'s, and had provided money for it, and as his indorsement was by way of guarantee, he was not injured by the delay; and that the request to send the

the notes to him was either a waiver of notice or notice by anticipation; but on a rule nisi to enter a nonsuit, and cause shewn, though he thought justice was clearly with the plaintiff, he thought he could not recover, for though the indorsement was by way of guarantee it was liable to all the legal consequences of an indorsement, and Gouthit's promise to pay was only to pay such as should be duly presented at Drury's. Judges Heath and Rooke were of the same opinion, and the rule was made absolute.

PROTEST.

Leftley v. *Mills*, 4 Term Rep. 170. An inland bill for 20*l*. 7*s*. payable fourteen days after sight, became due the 24th of April 1790. A banker's clerk called with it for payment in the morning, and the acceptor not being at home, left word where it lay; after six, another of the clerks, who was a Notary, noted it, and between seven and eight the first clerk went with it again; the acceptor tendered him the amount of the bill, and 6*d*. over, but he insisted on 2*s*. 6*d*. for the noting, and *that* sum not being paid, an action was brought against the acceptor, who pleaded the tender. Lord Kenyon thought a tender of the amount of the bill at any time of the day it was payable was sufficient, upon which the Jury found a verdict for the defendant. A rule to shew cause why there should not be a new trial was afterwards granted, and upon cause shewn Lord Kenyon thought the acceptor had till the last minute of the day of grace to pay the bill, and that it could not be noted or protested till the following day. Judge Buller thought bills were payable any time of the last day of grace upon demand, so as such

demand

demand was made within reasonable hours; and that they might be protested on that day. Judge Grose declined giving any opinion on these points; but the whole Court concurred that the bill in question could not be noted, because it was payable within a limited time *after sight*, and the statute authorises the noting of such inland bills only as are payable *after date*. Lord Kenyon also thought that the 6*d.* tendered was sufficient for the noting, and the rule was discharged.

Gale v. *Walsh*, 5 Term Rep. 239. In an action against the drawer of a foreign bill it was reserved as a point whether it was necessary to prove a protest; and the Court thought it so clear upon the motion to enter a nonsuit, that they suggested to the plaintiff's counsel the expediency of making the rule absolute in the first instance, and upon their acquiescence it was accordingly done; they afterwards, however, wished to have it opened, upon an idea that the drawer had no effects in the hands of the drawee; but it appearing upon the record that the idea was not founded, the rule stood. And in *Brough* v. *Parkins*, Lord Raym. 993. 6 Mod. 80. Salk. 131. Chief Justice Holt says, " A protest on a foreign bill is part of the custom."

Brough v. *Parkins*, Lord Raym. 992. 6 Mod. 80. Salk. 131. In an action against the drawer of an inland bill, it was insisted upon for error that it did not appear by the declaration that the bill had been protested; sed per Chief Justice Holt, " On an inland bill no protest was necessary by the common law, and the statute does not destroy or take away the party's action where there is no protest: nor is the want of a protest any bar of the action; but the act seems only to take away from the plaintiff

tiff his interest and damages where he has not made a protest, or to give the drawer a remedy against him by way of action for the costs and damages,"—and the judgment was affirmed.

Harris v. *Benson*, Str. 910. In an action against the drawer of an inland bill after an acceptance, Chief Justice Raymond ruled, that for want of a protest according to 9 & 10 Wm. 3. c. 17. the drawer could not be charged with interest.

RE-EXCHANGE.

Mellish v. *Simeon*, 2 H. Blackst. 378. A bill was drawn in London upon Paris, and negotiated through Holland; before it became due, the French Government prohibited the payment of any bill drawn in England, in consequence of which it was dishonoured, and sent back through the different hands by which it had before been negotiated, to London; the re-exchange between Paris and Holland raised the bill from 603*l*. 19*s*. 10*d*. to 905*l*. 13*s*. 9*d*. and the re-exchange between Holland and London to 913*l*. 4*s*. 3*d*. which the plaintiff (the payee) paid; and upon an action by him against the drawer Chief Justice Eyre left it to the Jury whether the defendant was liable for the re-exchange occasioned by returning the bill through Holland, and they found that he was. An application was made for a new trial, upon the ground that the defendant was not liable for the re-exchange, because there was no default in him, the payment being prohibited by the Government of France; but the Court held it immaterial why the bill was not paid; that as it was not paid he was liable to all the consequences, of which the re-exchange was one; and the rule was refused.

Auriol v. *Thomas*, 2 Term Rep. 52. Upon executing a writ of inquiry on a bill for the payment of 800 star pagodas returned protested from India, it appeared that the usage was to charge 10*s.* per pagoda for bills returned from India protested, and five per cent. after the expiration of thirty days from the notice to the defendant of the bill's dishonour, which included all incidental charges, and that the defendant had agreed to pay accordingly; upon which the Jury assessed the damages at 10*s.* per pagoda with the five per cent. though the plaintiff discounted the bill at the rate of 6*s.* 6*d.* a pagoda; that being then the current price. A rule nisi was obtained to set aside the inquisition on the ground that this allowance was exorbitant, and the agreement for it usurious; but the Court, on cause shewn, thought otherwise, and discharged the rule.

TRANSFER *of Negotiable Instruments.*

Hill v. *Lewis*, Salk. 132. Moor drew one note payable to the defendant, or his order, and another payable to him generally, without any words to make it assignable; the defendant indorsed them to Zouch and Zouch to the plaintiff; the first objection was, that the plaintiff had been guilty of laches, but the Jury thought he had not; and it was then urged that the second note was not assignable; and Chief Justice Holt agreed that the indorsement of this note did not make him that drew it chargeable to the indorsee, for the words " *or to his order*'*,* give authority to assign it by indorsement; but the indorsement of a note which has not these words is good so as to make the indorser chargeable to the indorsee.

Smallwood

Smallwood v. *Vernon*, Str. 478. In an action against the indorser of a note the declaration stated that he became chargeable according to the tenor of the indorsement; and it was objected that the indorsement might appoint the payment at a time different from that mentioned in the note; sed per Cur. if it did, it would charge the indorser, for every indorsement is the same as making a new note. Vide 2 Show. 501. Comb. 32. Skin. 255, 256. 342. 411. 3 Mod. 87. 12 Mod. 36. Ld. Raym. 181. 444. 744. Salk. 125. 132, 133. 3 Salk. 68. Str. 442. 479. 1 Atk. 282. 2 Atk. 102. Burr. 670. 675. Dougl. 613.

Peacock v. *Rhodes*, Dougl. 611—633. A bill was drawn by the Defendant payable to Ingham or order, Ingham indorsed it in blank, after which it was stolen; the plaintiff took it bona fide, and paid a valuable consideration for it, and acceptance and payment being refused, gave notice to the defendant, and brought this action. A case was reserved for the opinion of the Court, and it was contended that this bill was not to be considered as payable to bearer, and that the plaintiff had no better right upon it than the person of whom he took it; but the Court said there was no difference between a note indorsed in blank and one payable to bearer; and the plaintiff had judgment. *Francis* v. *Mott* N. P. before Ld. Mansfield cited Dougl. 612. was a similar case, and the Attorney General, who was for the defendant, after attempting unsuccessfully to shew that the plaintiff *knew* the bill was obtained unfairly, gave up the cause.

Smith v. *Clarke*, Peake 225. A bill was indorsed in blank by the payee, and after some other indorsements was indorsed to Jackson or order; Jackson sent it to Muir and Atkinson, but did not indorse it, and Muir and

Atkinson

Atkinson discounted it with the plaintiffs; the plaintiffs struck out all the indorsements except the first, which continued blank. This was an action against the acceptor, and it was objected that the plaintiffs could not recover without an indorsement by Jackson, but Lord Kenyon held otherwise, and the plaintiffs recovered. The plaintiffs afterwards proved that Jackson desired Muir and Atkinson to discount this bill, but Lord Kenyon thought the plaintiff's case made out without this evidence.

P. Wilmot, J. Burr. 1227. Blackst. 299. The payee may check the currency of a bill or note by giving a bare authority to receive the money, as " Pay to A for my use;" and per Lord Hardwicke, in *Snee* v. *Prescott*, 1 Atk. 249. Bills and notes are frequently indorsed in this manner, " Pray pay the money to my use," in order to prevent their being filled up with such an indorsement as passes the interest.

Ancher v. *Bank of England*, Dougl. 615. 637. A Bill was drawn by the plaintiffs upon Claus Heide and Co. payable to Jans Mœstue or order. Mœstue indorsed it to this effect, " The within must be credited to Captain M. L. Dahl, value on account," and sent it to Claus Heide and Co. who credited Dahl for the amount, and gave notice to Dahl and the plaintiffs that they had done so; an indorsement by Dahl was afterwards forged upon the bill, and the Bank discounted it. Claus Heide and Co. having become insolvent, Fulberg paid it for the honour of the plaintiffs, and upon the ground that the indorsement had restrained the negotiability of the bill, they brought an action for money had and received against the Bank. Lord Mansfield directed a nonsuit; but upon a rule to shew cause why there should not be a new trial, and cause
shewn,

shewn, Lord Mansfield and Judges Willes and Ashhurst
thought the indorsement restrictive, and that the plaintiffs were entitléd to recover; but Judge Buller thought
otherwise; upon which Lord Mansfield said, the whole
turned on the question, Whether the bill continued negotiable? and if they altered their opinion they would mention the case again, but it never was mentioned afterwards; and upon a new trial Lord Mansfield directed the
Jury to find for the plaintiffs, which they did.

Moore v. *Manning*, Com. 311. A note was drawn by
the defendant payable to Statham or order: Statham indorsed it to Witherhead, but did not add " or to his order," and Witherhead indorsed it to the plaintiff. The
defendant contended that as there were no express words
to authorise Witherhead to assign it, he had no such
power, but the whole Court resolved that as the bill was
at first assignable by Statham as being payable to him or
order, and as all Statham's interest was transferred to
Witherhead, the right of assigning it was transferred
also, and the plaintiff had judgment.

Hawkins v. *Cardy*, Ld. Raym. 360. Carth. 466. 12
Mod. 213. Salk. 65. In an action upon a bill drawn by
the defendant for 46*l.* 19*s.* payable to Blackman or order
the declaration stated that Blackman indorsed 43*l.* 4*s.* of
it to the plaintiff; the defendant pleaded an insufficient
plea, upon which the plaintiff demurred, but the whole
Court held the declaration bad, because the bill could
not be indorsed for less than all the money due thereon
and the plaintiff discontinued his action. And per Judge
Gould, in *Johnson* v. *Kennion*, 2 Wils. 262. where the
drawer of a bill has paid part you may indorse it over
for the residue; otherwise not, because it would subject
him to a variety of actions.

Russel

Russel v. *Langstaff*, Doug. 496. 514. The defendant to accommodate Galley indorsed his name on five copper-plate checks, made in the form of promissory notes, but in blank, without any sums, dates, or times of payment being mentioned therein, and delivered them to Galley; Galley filled them up as he thought fit, and the plaintiff discounted them; the plaintiff knew the notes were blank at the time of the indorsement; Galley not paying them when they became due the plaintiff brought this action. Baron Hotham, before whom the cause was tried, was of opinion, that as the notes were incomplete when the defendant indorsed them, no subsequent act of Galley could make them otherwise, because that would alter the effect of the defendant's indorsement, and he accordingly directed a verdict for the defendant ; but upon an application for a new trial, and cause shewn, Mr. Wallace, the Attorney General, gave up the point, though Mr. Lee afterwards argued it, and Lord Mansfield said, " Nothing is so clear as the point; the indorsement on a blank note is a letter of credit for an indefinite sum; the defendant said, trust Galley to any amount, and I will be his security; it does not lie in his mouth to say the indorsements were not regular." A new trial was accordingly granted, and a verdict having been found for the plaintiff in a similar action before Lord Mansfield, the defendant submitted in this, without going to a second trial.

TRANSFER *in case of* DEATH.

Rawlinson v. *Stone*, 3 Wils. 1 Str. 1260. 2 Burr. 157. A note was payable to A B or order; A B died intestate, and

and his administrator indorsed it to the plaintiff. These facts appearing upon the declaration, the defendant demurred, and contended that the personal representative of the payee had no power to indorse a note, but the Court of Common Pleas, after three arguments, and the court of King's Bench upon error brought, were unanimously of opinion that he had, and each Court said it was every day's practice, and the constant usage for executors and administrators to indorse bills and notes payable to the order of the testators or intestates.

King v. *Thomas,* 1 Term Rep. 487. The Court held that upon a bill payable to several as executors, they might sue as executors; and per Judge Buller, no inconvenience can arise from their indorsing the bill; for if they indorse they are liable personally, and not as executors; for their indorsement would not give an action against the effects of the testator.

Transfer *in case of* Marriage.

Connor v. *Martin,* Str. 516. cited 3 Wils. 5. A bill was made payable to Susan Connor or order, while she was sole: she afterwards married; and during her coverture indorsed it to the plaintiff, and upon demurrer and argument the Court of Common Pleas held, that the feme covert could not assign the note, because by the marriage it became the sole right and property of the husband; and by Chief Justice Parker, in *Miles* v. *Williams,* 10 Mod. 246, if a note be payable to a feme sole or order, and she marry, her husband is the proper person to indorse it.

ANALYSIS

OF A

COUNT IN ASSUMPSIT

UPON A

Foreign Bill.

[LAST INDORSER AGAINST THE DRAWEES, OR FIRST INDORSERS.]

London } John Mills complains of Thomas Roper and Ste-
to wit. } phen Howe being, &c.—For that whereas on
(1) the 1st day of January 1789, at (2) London aforesaid,

    1 " On" &c. Upon a bill or note importing to be payable
within a limited time after the date, and dated on a particular
day, this * must be that day: on a bill or note importing to be
payable within a limited time after the date, and not dated, the
day † it issued, if it can be ascertained, otherwise ‡ the first day
the plaintiff knew and can prove that it existed.

    2 "At" &c. On a foreign bill this must be the place at which
it bears date; but where the drawing of the bill must be proved
upon a trial, some place in England or Wales should be subjoined under a videlicet, thus, " at Venice in Italy, to wit, at
London," &c.

    In

---

* *Stafford* v. *Forcer,* 10 *Mod.* 511. *cited Str.* 22.

† *Bayley, p.* 68, *note* (*a*).

‡ *Vide Beawes,* § 190, *p.* 439. [Mar. 91. 2d edit. 2 Ld. Raym.
1076. 4 T. R. 337. Bac. Abr. tit. *Leases,* L. 1. Com. Dig. tit.
Fait. B. 3.]

said, in the parish of St. Mary le Bow, in the ward of Cheap, certain persons using the stile and firm (*a*) of Gaunt and Co. according (3) to the usage and custom of merchants from time immemorial used and approved of, made (4) their certain Bill of Exchange in writing, their (5) copartnership, stile, and firm aforesaid being thereunto subscribed,

In an action against the drawer, the want of subjoining such place may be taken advantage of by special demurrer to the count, but by special demurrer* only.

Inland bills and notes, though they may bear date at a particular place, may be alleged to have been made any where in England or Wales.

A bill or note made by a servant may be stated to have been made by the master, because that † is its legal operation.

3 "According" &c. It is ‡ not requisite to set out any part of the custom, and even a reference to it is § unnecessary.

In actions upon notes, instead of referring to the custom of merchants, the count refers to the statute.

4. " Made." Where a man signs his name upon a blank paper, stamped with a bill stamp, and delivers it to another to draw above the signature what bill he pleases thereon, and he draws one accordingly, the || bill may be stated to have been made by the person whose signature it bears.

5. " Their," &c. A signature, when essential, is ¶ implied by the

* *Vide* 16 &' 17 *Car. II. c.* 8. § 1. 4 *Anne c.* 16. § 1.

† *Vide Bayley p.* 103.

‡ *Soper* v. *Dible, Lord Raym.* 175. [2 Ld. Raym. 88. 1542. Bayl. 55.]

§ *Erskine* v. *Murray, Lord Raym.* 1542.

|| *Collis* v. *Emett*, 1 *H. Blackst.* 313.

¶ *Elliot* v. *Cooper, Lord Raym.* 1376. [1484. 1542.]

(*a*) [" Firm." An indorsement by one of a firm in his name and company, is good to bind the other partners, though the firm has always been known by the name of another partner and company, subscribed, bearing (6) date the day and year aforesaid, and (7) directed to one Henry Hunt, at Venice, in Italy, in parts beyond the seas, and (8) thereby requested the said Henry, at double usance, to pay that their first of exchange

the preceding word " made;" this allegation, therefore, is not strictly necessary.

6. " Bearing," &c. This allegation * also may be dispensed with; for it shall be intended, when the date is material, that a bill or note was dated when drawn.

7. " Directed," &c. In an action against the acceptor upon a bill directed to him, or in his absence to I. S. the † conditional direction to I. S. need not be stated.

8. " Thereby," &c. A bill or note may be stated according to its legal operation.

Thus a joint or several note, or a note importing in the body of it to be made by several persons, but signed by one only, may be ‡ stated as a several note.

Nay, where the plaintiff in an action against one of two makers of a joint or several note, stated that the defendant and another made their certain note, &c. and thereby jointly or severally promised to pay, the Court held it § well after judgment by default, notwithstanding as the truth of either member verifies a disjunctive proposition, the note might have been joint.

And in an ‖ action against one of the several makers of a joint note, if it be stated as a several one, the objection can only be taken by plea in abatement.

A bill or note importing to be payable to a fictitious person

may

* *De la Courtier* v. *Bellamy*, 2 *Show.* 422.

† *Anon.* 12 *Mod.* 447.

‡ *Roberts* v. *Peake*, *Burr.* 323.

§ *Butler* v. *Malissy*, *Str.* 76.

‖ *Rees* v. *Abbott*, *Cowp.* 832.

company, unless it be shewn that there is such a distinct house as that by the style of which the indorsement is made. 1 New-York T. R. 184.]

exchange (second (9) and third of the same tenor not paid)
to the said Thomas and Stephen, or (10) their order, a
certain sum of foreign money called in the said bill seven
hundred

may be stated to be payable to the person in whose favour the
indorsement is made to * bearer.

A bill or note intended to have been made payable to A. that
he might guarantee the payment to B. but through ignorance or
mistake made payable to B. and by him indorsed to A. and then
indorsed back by A. to B. may be† stated to have been made payable to A.

The payee of a bill or note payable " to his order," may ‡ state
it to have been made payable to himself.

9. " Second," &c. In an action upon a bill consisting of several parts, if the plaintiff has each part, it may be doubted whether he need take notice of this condition, because all the parts
collectively make an unconditional bill; and where he has not
each part, it should seem more correct to state that the drawer
made his certain bill of exchange in writing in three parts, his
proper hand being subscribed to each of the said parts, bearing
date, &c. and directed, &c. and by one of the said parts requested, &c. but the form adopted by Bayley is the usual one.

10. " Or order," &c. In an action by the assignee of a bill or
note, it is necessary to shew that the bill or note authorises a
transfer, in an action by the payee, § not.

* *Bayley p.* 11, *note (a)*.
† *Bishop* v. *Hayward,* 4 *T. R.* 470.
‡ *Frederick* v. *Cotton,* 2 *Show.* 8.
§ *Vide Bayley p.* 11, *note (a)*.

hundred ducats, value received,(*b*) and then and there delivered the said bill to the said Thomas and Stephen, which
(11) said bill the said Henry Hunt afterwards, to wit, on
(12) the day and year aforesaid, at Venice, to wit, at London aforesaid, in the parish and ward aforesaid, on sight
thereof, duly according to the usage and custom of merchants accepted, and the said Thomas and Stephen afterwards and before [time appointed for] the payment of the
said sum of money in the said bill mentioned, or of any
part thereof, to wit on the day and year aforesaid, at London aforesaid, in the parish and ward aforesaid, by their
certain indorsement in writing then and there made upon
the said bill, their proper hands being thereunto subscribed,
according to the usage and custom of merchants appointed the (13) contents of the said bill to be paid to one Peter

11. "Which," &c. Except in actions against acceptors, or on
bills payable within a limited time after sight, the acceptance
need not be stated.

12. "On," &c. Where the time of payment depends on the
presentment, this should be the very day of presentment; in
other cases exactness as to the day is not requisite.

If however the plaintiff allege in terms that the acceptance
was made before the time limited by a bill for its payment, it has
been laid down that he will be * precluded from giving in evidence
an acceptance afterwards, but this may perhaps be doubted.

13. "The contents." On an indorsement for less than the full
sum mentioned in the bill or note, the plaintiff must † shew that
the residue was paid.

* *Jackson* v. *Pigott*, *Lord Raym.* 364.
† *Hawkins* v. *Gardner*, 12 *Mod.* 213.

(*b*) [These words, *value received*, are implied in every bill and
indorsement, 2 Show. 496. Bayl. 13. n. a. Ld. Raym. 1481.
Fort. 282. Lutw. 889. 3 Wils. 212. 2 Stra. 1212. *Semb. contra.*
vid.

ter White, or (14) his order, and then and there delivered the said bill so indorsed to the said Peter, and (15) the said Peter afterwards, and before the payment of the said sum of money in the said bill mentioned, or of any part thereof, to wit, on the day and year aforesaid, at London aforesaid, in the parish and ward aforesaid, by his certain indorsement in writing then and there made upon the said bill, his proper hand being thereunto subscribed, appointed the contents of the said bill to be paid to the said John, and then and there delivered the said bill so indorsed to the said John, of (16) which said indorsements the said Henry, afterwards to wit, on the day and year aforesaid,

14. " Or his Order." These *words are unnecessary.

A full and blank indorsement are stated in the same manner.

15. " And the said Peter," &c. Every indorsement essential to a transfer must be stated: unnecessary one may † be omitted.

Where the plaintiff would omit an indorsement, he should represent that which precedes it to have been made in favour of the person who is indorsee upon that which follows.

Thus if a bill payable to Allen's order be indorsed by him in blank, and delivered to Bradley, and indorsed by Bradley to Carter, if Carter would omit stating Bradley's indorsement, he should state that Allen indorsed it immediately to him.

16. " Of which," &c. This ‡ allegation is unnecessary.

* Vide Bayley p. 12.   † Peacock v. Rhodes, Bayley p. 32.

‡ Anon. Pract. Reg. 358.

vid. Chitty 50. But to entitle the holder to recover interest and damages against the drawer and indorser, in default of acceptance or payment, a bill must contain the words, *value received,* 9 & 10 W. 3. c. 17.;3 & 4 Ann. 9. s. 4]

aforesaid, at London aforesaid, in the parish and ward aforesaid, had notice; and the said John in fact says, that (17) an usance mentioned in any bill of exchange drawn in London and payable in Venice, is, and at the several times aforesaid was, three months from the date of the said bill, and no other time whatever; and (18) that

17. " That an usance," &c. A neglect to shew the duration of an usance is fatal * upon demurrer (unless perhaps where it is alleged that the bill was presented on the day it was payable), but upon demurrer only.†

18. " And that," &c. In an action against the maker of a note or the acceptor of a bill (except on an ‡ acceptance at the house of a stranger), the presentment is never stated.

In an action against the drawer of a bill, or the indorser of a bill or note, it is essential to state either that the § bill or note was presented, that the ‖ drawee or maker could not be found, or that the defendant, had he paid the bill, would have had no remedy against them.

If the drawee or maker cannot be found it is ¶ sufficient to aver generally that he was not found, without stating that any inquiry was made after him.

On an allegation that the bill or note was presented, and acceptance or payment refused, the plaintiff cannot give ** in evidence that the drawee or maker could not be found.

In

* *Buckley* v. *Campbell*, *Salk.* 131.
† *Smart* v. *Dean*, 3 *Keb.* 645.
‡ *Bishop* v. *Chitty*, *Bayley* 78, note (*a*).
§ *Mercer* v. *Southwell*, 2 *Show.* 180.
‖ *Bayley p.* 58.
¶ *Starke* v. *Cheeseman*, *Carth.* 509.
** *R. Leeson* v. *Pigott*, *Sittings after Trinity* 1788

that afterwards, and when the said bill had, according
to the tenor and effect thereof, become payable, to wit
on (19) the fourth day of July in the year aforesaid, at
Venice aforesaid, to wit, at London aforesaid, in the parish and ward aforesaid, the said bill was duly, according
to the usage and custom of merchants, shewn and presented to the said Henry for payment; and the said
Henry was then and there requested to pay the said sum
of money in the said bill mentioned, but the said Henry
did not then or there pay the said sum of money in the
said bill mentioned, or any part thereof, but wholly
neglected and refused so to do; neither (20) did he pay
the said second or third of exchange in the said bill mentioned, or either of them: nor (21) did the said persons
so using the stile and firm of Gaunt and Co. pay the said
sum of money in the said bill mentioned, or any part
thereof,

In an action against the acceptor of a bill or maker of a note
payable on demand, a * presentment need not be stated.

19. " On," &c. Unless there is an express averment that the
presentment was made on the day when the bill or note became
payable, this † must be that very day; where there is such averment, exactness as to the day is immaterial.

20. " Neither," &c. Where the plaintiff states that the sum
of money mentioned in the bill was not paid, this allegation is
not ‡ necessary.

21. " Nor," &c. This § allegation is unnecessary.

* *Rumball* v. *Ball*, 10 *Mod.* 38.
† *Rushton* v. *Aspinall*, *Bayley p.* 109.
‡ *Starke* v. *Cheeseman*, *Carth.* 509.
§ *Vide Bayley* c. 6.

thereof, or the said second or third of exchange; and thereupon the said John, afterwards to wit on the day and year last aforesaid, at Venice aforesaid, to wit at London aforesaid, in the parish and ward aforesaid, according to the usage and custom of merchants, caused the said bill to be protested (22) for non-payment, of all which premises the said Thomas and Stephen afterwards to wit, on the day and year last aforesaid, at London aforesaid, in the parish and ward aforesaid, had (23) notice; and by reason thereof, and by force of the usage and custom of merchants, became liable to pay to (24) the said John the said sum of money in the

said

22. " Protested," &c. The protest * need not be stated in an action on an inland bill; in an action on a foreign one the plaintiff † must either state it or ‡ shew that it was not necessary; but the omission § can only be taken advantage of by a special demurrer.

In stating the protest if the plaintiff allege, " *that he protested the bill, or caused it to be protested,*" it will be unobjectionable if the defendant pleads over.

23. " Notice." If the defendant is prima facie entitled to notice, it is essentially necessary to state that he had ‖ notice, or to shew that he was not entitled thereto. [Want of funds in the hands of the drawee will excuse want of notice. 1 New York T. R. 157. Chitty 102.]

24. " To the said John." In an action upon a bill or note stated upon the count to be payable to the order of

the

* See *Brough* v. *Parkins, Bayley p.* 75, *note* (b).

† *Solomons* v. *Staveley, cited Dougl. 2d edit.* 684, n. 144.

‡ *Rogers* v. *Stephens, Bayley p.* 78, *note* (d).

§ *Witherby* v. *Sarsfield,* 1 *Show.* 125.　　‖*Rushton* v. *Aspinall, Bayl. p.* 109.

said bill mentioned, or the value thereof, when (25) they the said Thomas and Stephen should be thereunto afterwards requested: and (26) being so liable, they the said Thomas and Stephen, in consideration thereof afterwards to wit on the day and year last aforesaid, at London aforesaid, in the parish and ward aforesaid, undertook, and to the said John then and there faithfully promised to pay to him the said sum of money in the said bill mentioned, or the value thereof, when they the said Thomas and Stephen should be thereunto afterwards requested:

the plaintiff, it is sometimes * usual, though † unnecessary, to insert here an allegation that the plaintiff made no order ; but the † better way upon a bill or note made so payable is, to state according to the legal operation that it was made payable to the plaintiff, and then this allegation would be impertinent.

25. " When," &c. In an action against the acceptor of a bill or maker of a note not payable immediately upon presentment, instead of alleging that the defendant became liable, and promised to pay *when he should be thereunto afterwards requested*, he is stated to have become liable, and promised to pay *according to the tenor and effect of the bill and acceptance* in the one case, and *of the note* in the other.

26. " And," &c. This clause is unnecessary in an action against either the ‡ acceptor of a bill or the maker of a note ; and it may be doubted whether || it is essential in any other.

* *Fisher* v. *Pomfret, Carth.* 403.
† *Vide Frederick* v. *Cotton, Bayley p.* 105, *note* (c).
‡ *Wegersloffe* v. *Keene, Str.* 114.
|| *Starke* v. *Cheeseman, Carth.* 509. *Salk.* 128.

requested: and (27) the said John avers, that the said seven hundred ducats in the said bill mentioned, on the day and year last aforesaid were, and from thenceforth hitherto have been and still are of great value, to wit of the value of ————*l.* of lawful money of Great Britain, that is to say at London aforesaid, in the parish and ward aforesaid; yet the said Thomas and Stephen (although often requested) have not, nor hath either of them paid to the said John the said sum of money in the said bill mentioned, or any part thereof, or the value thereof, or of any part thereof, but hath wholly neglected, and refused, and still neglects and refuses so to do; wherefore the said John says he is injured, and hath sustained damage to the value of ————*l.* and therefore he brings suit, &c.

27. " And the said," &c. This averment is never necessary; the* want of it is certainly cured by verdict.

* *Simmonds* v. *Parminter,* 1 *Wils.* 185.

NOTARIAL

NOTARIAL FEES OF OFFICE.

As settled the 1st of July 1797, by a Meeting of the principal Bankers, Merchants, and Notaries, at the George and Vulture.

	£.	s.	d.
NOTING—Bills drawn upon or addressed at the house of persons residing within the ancient walls of the city of London	0	1	6
—— If without the said walls, and not exceeding the under-mentioned limits*	0	2	6
—— If off the pavement, additional per mile	0	1	6

* Bills drawn upon or addressed at the house of any persons residing between Old or New Bond Street, Wimpole Street, New Cavendish Street, Upper Marybone Street, Howland Street, Lower Gower Street, lower end of Gray's Inn Lane, and not off the Pavement, Clerkenwell Church, Old Street, Shoreditch Church, Brick Lane, St. George's in the East, Execution Dock, Wapping, Dock Head, upper end of Bermondsey Street as far as the Church, end of Blackman Street, end of Great Surry Street, Blackfriar's Road as far as the Circus, Cuper's Bridge, Bridge Street Westminster, Abington Street, Piccadilly, and the like distances, 3s. 6d.

PROTESTING—Bills drawn upon or
addressed at the house of any persons residing *within the ancient
walls* of London (including the
stamp duty of 4*s.* and exclusive
of the charge of noting)   -   0 6 6
—— If *without the walls* (including
the stamp duty, and exclusive
of noting), agreeable to the distances subjoined   -   0 8 0

ACTS OF HONOUR—*Within* the ancient walls of London, upon each 0 1 6
——*Without* ditto, conformable to
the second article, and the distances subjoined; and the like
charge for any additional demand that may be made upon
the said bill.

POST DEMANDS and acts thereof
within the City of London - 0 2 6
——Without, if registered only in
the Notary's books   -   0 3 6
*And in the same proportion with respect to dis-
tance as in Noting.*

Copy of Bill paid in part, with receipt at the foot thereof   -   0   2   0

*And in the same proportion for every additional
bill so copied, exclusive of Receipt Stamps.*

Duplicate Protests each (including 4*s.* for duty)   -   0   7   6
For every additional bill (exclusive
of duty) -   -   -   0   3   6

Translations—Every folio of
ninety words translated from the
French, Dutch, or Flemish into
English -   -   -   0   1   6
—— English into French, Dutch, or
Flemish, *per folio*   -   0   1   9
—— English into Italian, Spanish,
Portuguese, German, Danish,
and Swedish, *per folio*   -   0   3   0
—— Latin into English, *per folio*   0   2   6
Attesting same as true (exclusive of
stamps and attendance)   -   0   7   6

City Seals—Each, if only one deponent, exclusive of exemplification 1   1   0
—— Each additional deponent in the
affidavit   0   10   6

NOTARIAL COPIES *per folio* of seventy-two words, exclusive of attestation, stamps, &c. - - -

TABLE OF STAMPS.

Bills or Notes on Demand.

5*l*. 5*s*.	0	0	6	50*l*. to 100*l*.	0	2	0
5*l*. 5*s*. to 30*l*.	0	1	0	100*l*. to 200*l*.	0	3	0
30*l*. to 50*l*.	0	1	6	Above 200*l*.	0	4	0

Bills or Notes after Date.

40*s*. to 30*l*.	0	1	0	50*l*. to 100*l*.	0	2	0
30*l*. to 50*l*.	0	1	6	100*l*. to 200*l*.	0	3	0
	200*l*. and upwards	0	4	0			

Bills of Exchange drawn in sets.

100*l*. or under, each	0	1	1
100*l*. to 200*l*.	0	1	6
Above 200*l*.	0	2	0

EXEMPT.

Drafts and Orders payable on Demand, dated the day before issuing the same, and drawn upon any Banker, and all Notes of the Bank of England.

Money Bonds.

If 100*l*. or under	0	15	0	1000*l*. to 2000*l*.	2	0	0
100*l*. to 500*l*.	1	0	0	2000*l*. to 5000*l*.	3	0	0
500*l*. to 1000*l*.	1	10	0	5000*l*. and upwards	5	0	0

Receipts.

40*s*. to under 20*l*.	0	0	2	50*l*. to under 100*l*.		0	6
20*l*. to under 50*l*.	0	0	4	100*l*. to under 500*l*.	0	1	0
	500*l*. and upwards, in full	0	2	0			

POSTAGE BY THE GENERAL POST.

Distances.		single	double	treble	ounce
15 miles		0 3	0 6	0 9	1 0
15 and not exceeding	30	0 4	0 8	1 0	1 4
30	50	0 5	0 10	1 3	1 8
50	80	0 6	1 0	1 6	2 0
80	120	0 7	1 2	1 9	2 4
120	170	0 8	1 4	2 0	2 8
170	230	0 9	1 6	2 3	3 0
230	300	0 10	1 8	2 6	3 4
Every 100 above 300 add.		0 1	0 2	0 3	0 4
Foreign Letters additional		0 4	0 8	1 0	1 4
Irish Letters additional		0 2	0 4	0 6	0 8

THE END.

www.ingramcontent.com/pod-product-compliance
Lightning Source LLC
Chambersburg PA
CBHW031420180326
41458CB00002B/451